ROOTS
OF PEACE

ROOTS OF PEACE

The Movement Against Militarism in Canada

Edited by Eric Shragge, Ronald Babin,

and Jean-Guy Vaillancourt

©Between The Lines 1986

Published by Between The Lines,
            229 College St.,
            Toronto, Ontario
            M5T 1R4

Typeset by Alphabets Inc.
Cover by Goodness Graphics
Printed by Les Editions Marquis Ltée

Between The Lines is a joint project of Dumont Press Graphix,
Kitchener, and the Development Education Centre, Toronto. It receives
financial assistance from the Canada Council and the Ontario Arts
Council.

Canadian Cataloguing in Publication Data

Main entry under title:

Roots of peace

Bibliography: p.
ISBN 0-919946-74-7 (bound) ISBN 0-919946-75-5 (pbk.)

1. Peace. 2. Disarmament. 3. Canada – Foreign relations.
I. Shragge, Eric, 1948-   . II. Babin, Ronald. III. Vaillancourt,
Jean-Guy.

JX1952.R66 1986   327.1'72'0971   C86-094648-7

Table of Contents

Part Two: Organizing for Peace

Acknowledgements

This book grew out of an earlier project involving many writers and activists in the peace movement. In autumn 1984 *Revue internationale
d'action communautaire* (RIAC) published a special issue edited by Jean-
Guy Vaillancourt and Ronald Babin and containing 26 articles in French
on the international movement for disarmament and peace. Originally we
thought that an English translation of this RIAC issue would make a
useful contribution to the ongoing discussion around the role of the peace
movement in Canada, but as it developed the project turned into
something quite different. Although a number of the RIAC articles remain
in this book, they have been not only translated but also substantially
revised. We have also added new articles, most of them previously unpublished, on Canada's links to the arms race in an international context,
and on the various roles and shapes of the Canadian peace movement.

The articles originally published in RIAC (12/52, automne 1984) are:
Dan Smith, "Le mouvement européen pour le désarmement nucléaire et le
non-alignement"; David Mandel (Seppo), "L'URSS et le mouvement
pour le désarmement et la paix"; Pierre Beaudet, "Pour un véritable
'dialogue Nord-Sud', ou la rencontre nécessaire entre les mouvements
pour la paix et les mouvements de libération"; Phyllis Aronoff,
"Militarisme et pacifisme: un approche féministe"; and Eric Shragge, "Le
mouvement canadien pour la paix: dans ou contre l'Etat".

Three of the articles included—"Towards a True North-South Dialogue", "Non-Alignment and Detente from Below", and "A Feminist Approach to Militarism and Peace"—were ably translated by Phyllis Aronoff and Howard Scott. The other articles that originated in French were translated and/or reworked by the authors.

One article, "The Empire Strikes Back" by Bryan Palmer, was originally published in *Studies in Political Economy: A Socialist Review*, No. 12, Fall 1983. Bryan Palmer wrote this article in 1983 and the views therein, he notes, do not necessarily reflect his current thinking and political perspective. We are grateful to *Studies in Political Economy* for giving us permission to reprint this article.

We thank all of the authors for their contributions to this volume. Most of them have been active in the peace movement in one way or another, and the book represents their concern to help develop the analysis that must go hand in hand with activism. They share in common the belief that the peace movement plays a crucial role in raising alternatives to the status quo of militarism, patriarchy, and Cold War politics. The hope for this book is that those active in issues of disarmament, militarism, and international politics—as well as those simply concerned about these questions—will use the articles as tools not only for reflection but also for moving the ongoing debate towards a stronger consensus and a new vision for Canada—one that stands for peace and justice.

Eric Shragge, Ronald Babin, and Jean-Guy Vaillancourt
Montreal, August 1986

Introduction

Eric Shragge, Ronald Babin, and
Jean-Guy Vaillancourt

THE NEW GENERATION of the Canadian peace movement was born in the early 1980s and grew rapidly, especially over the issue of Cruise missile testing. Demonstrations, petitions, public education, and acts of civil disobedience polarized a national debate, brought new adherents, and opened the minds of many to the antinuclear position. Although there was not a co-ordinated national campaign, a sense of movement and public protest developed around this issue. The tensions and insecurities brought about by the "New Cold War", the bellicose rhetoric of Reagan, the massive protests in Europe, and the destabilization of the precarious nuclear balance sparked concern for many Canadians. Cruise testing, rather than being only a technical exercise, presented a test of Canada's loyalty to the American empire.

Although the peace movement lost this issue, important consequences resulted. The lack of a central organization or campaign directorate (up until the Peace Petition Caravan Campaign in 1984) brought the responsibility for organizing down to the local level. Hundreds of local groups and even more initiatives emerged. As well, larger organizations and other movements brought the peace question onto their own agendas. Disarmament became an important part of the women's movement, churches, trade unions, and professional groupings. Networking between groups organized actions at the city, regional, and provincial levels. More recently a national network of groups, the Canadian Peace Alliance, was founded.

Thus, out of a defeat, and a loosely organized national movement, a peace presence developed in Canada. The movement also made other inroads at the level of popular beliefs. The ideological underpinnings supporting the necessity of nuclear escalation—for example, that a nuclear war can be limited and winnable, that more nuclear arms bring more security, that the USSR is the permanent enemy and can only be dealt with by force—have been challenged. Discussions and debates around Canada's involvement in NATO have begun, although timidly. The emergence of this wave of disarmament activity, crystallized by Cruise testing, has put the peace question back onto the political agenda and the movement has taken some large steps forward.

This book is a result of reflection and action. It is a product of individuals involved in different aspects of disarmament activity over the last few years. Although the contributors do not share identical perspectives, there are certain common strands. There is a belief that the peace movement has to challenge power in Canadian society, and that this challenge cannot be limited to attempts to influence politicians. If Canadians want their government to play a different role in the world, especially in relation to the roles of the United States and the Soviet Union, relations of power tied in to the arms race need to be challenged. This can only take place "from below" through individuals and groups taking the initiative and leading the politicians, and this push must begin with a more critical view and understanding of Canada's role, and a wider critique of international relations.

In order to become long-term and viable, the peace movement has to confront the roots of the arms race as it appears in the Canadian context and present concrete alternatives. This means that we must go beyond a minimalist program, such as opposition to Cruise testing and Star Wars, and open up debate on the underpinnings. This book tries to do just that. As well, to varying degrees, authors in this volume are sceptical about the use of the structures and institutions of the state to make the necessary changes. For many in the peace movement, the content of this book may be a departure from ideas and strategies pursued over the last few years. It is the hope that the perspective here breathes fresh air into the debate, moves the movement along in its struggle.

The book's first part examines Canada in a wider international context. Canada has presented itself to the world as a moderate, peace-loving nation, committed to peacekeeping and international mediation. These beliefs, particularly under the Mulroney government, have been proven false again and again, especially as Canada quickly jumps to the defence of

U.S. actions such as its challenge to the Salt II agreements, the renewal of the stockpiling of chemical weapons, or the bombing of Libya. These positions follow an historic pattern. Since the end of World War II, Canada has adhered to basic U.S. assumptions on foreign policy issues as its friendly neighbour rose to become the leading capitalist nation and the architect of Cold War politics. Canadian governments have shared the U.S. viewpoint that the permanent enemies are the USSR and the threat of world communism. As a participant in the world economic order, Canadian capital shares similar economic interests and needs with that of U.S. capital. Corporations participate in a global market, and Canadian capital is smaller but not insignificant in the exploitation of this market.[1] If Canada is to play a role in moving towards a more peaceful world, the peace movement needs to confront the centrality of Canada-U.S. relations, and Canada's role as a less shrill cold warrior. These are issues taken up in the articles by Leonard Johnson and Bryan Palmer.

Two other international issues are central: relations with the Third World, and "What About the Russians?". The peace movement has confronted and debated the nuclear question, which—although it does have basic consequences for developing countries—is mainly an issue of the North. On the other hand, actual wars and struggles for justice and wars of national liberation are being fought out in the Third World. These wars and struggles have become proxies for the superpowers, whether in Central America, Africa, Southeast Asia, or Afghanistan. Pierre Beaudet raises crucial questions around the issues of the North-South relationship and argues the importance of developing a strategy that takes this relationship into account.

The propaganda and very existence of the Western alliance (NATO), including Canada as a staunch supporter, are based on the idea that the USSR is not only a present danger to the West but is also our permanent enemy. No matter how we may argue to the contrary, we must deal with the facts: It is the missiles of the USSR that are pointing at us. How can we explain these issues in a way that is critical of the USSR—its contribution to the arms race, its repression at home, and its military activities in its region—without falling into Cold War posturing? How do we deal with its recent peace initiatives and unilateral moritorium on nuclear testing? The essay by David Mandel takes up this challenge.

One of the more interesting aspects of the current peace movement is its approach to moving beyond bloc politics and its practice of internationalism. One of the themes that is taken up in a number of essays is that Canada should move to a non-aligned position vis à vis the two superpowers. This would constitute a major step forward in extricating Canada from the blocs and in developing alternative positions in an increasingly polarized world. Dan Smith clearly sets out the arguments for non-alignment, reflecting on the situation in Europe and drawing important lessons for Canadians.

Internationalism in practice has moved beyond vague gestures and formal exchanges between the blocs, initiated by groups and individuals. It has begun to develop into networks of co-operation, solidarity, and to a limited extent a shared world view. The practice of the North Atlantic Network provides a good example of how peace groups from several nations and regions can work together in a non-hierarchical way on issues of common concern. Groups have come together to discuss the militarization of the Atlantic, to develop analysis, take actions on common themes, and generally work as an international support network.[2] This form of internationalism represents a form of "alliances" from below—between Western activists.

Another form of internationalism can be described as "detente from below". It began with Western peace activists and groups setting up support for independent peace activists and groups in Eastern bloc countries and fighting against the repression of these activities. An important dialogue and debate and in Europe a partial convergence of vision have emerged, transcending bloc politics. These issues are discussed in the essay by Babin, Shragge, and Beaudet.

The first part of this book, then, attempts to bring an internationalist perspective to Canadian peace activism, and to locate Canada in a wider context. It attempts to examine the constraints of bloc politics on Canada, and the need for the peace movement to develop an international and long-term vision of peace and the role for Canada. The second part looks at approaches taken by peace activists, and some issues faced by the peace movement.

The themes are varied. One of the most important involves the way that disarmament has been taken up as an issue by the women's movement, the trade unions, and how it has made links to urban reform movements. The articles by Phyllis Aronoff, Andrea Levy, Marion Kerans, and Eric Shragge and David Mandel deal with these developments. They illustrate that with this bridging of movements the peace question has been given greater strength and organizational support than it would have had if the issues had remained exclusively in peace groups. The questions have been broadened beyond weapons and their use and include the connections between militarism and violence against women, and between employment and the conversion of military to socially useful goods. The questions include the role of direct democracy and expression on larger international questions at the local, municipal level.

Gordon Edwards's article examines the uranium trade and through it one of Canada's main contributions to nuclear weapons. This is a central issue for peace activists, and it links those in the ecology movement who oppose nuclear energy with those working on the peace question. In the important area of strategy for the peace movement, Paul Cappon presents examples of his experiences lobbying government officials, and critiques this approach, showing its limitations and arguing that the push has to come from below, from an informed active population. The last article by the book's co-editors attempts to look at some of the content and organizational issues that the movement will face in coming years. We do this not as a preformulated program but rather as a means of stimulating debate on direction and organization.

The central theme in this collection is that Canada's role in the arms race cannot be separated from basic relations of power in our society. Central, of course, is our participation in the Western alliance, and our relation with the United States. Our foreign and defence policy is fundamentally shaped by this relation. Not only does this lead to events such as Cruise testing, but it defines what goods get produced, through agreements such as the Defense Production Sharing Arrangement, directly determining employment patterns in certain regions. The intermeshing of Canada and the United States is not only related to foreign policy and armament production but also involves other issues such as free trade and cultural autonomy. It is not within the scope of this book to raise these issues, except to state that until Canada moves in a direction of autonomy and away from the United States on domestic and foreign policy, and even though the peace movement may play a constructive role in our society and limit some aspects of the arms race, we shall continue to replay conflicts on specific issues time and time again. Canada will only be a country for peace when it can become independent enough from U.S. interests to push forward, in conjunction with other nations, policies and approaches that make concrete moves towards disarmament and therefore international security.

Power relations that produce militarism do not only come from outside Canada. Capital accumulation, the drive of private enterprise for profit, is a central feature of our society. It pays little heed to morality and turns in the direction of profit. If manufacturing arms is profitable regardless of their destination or use, these investments will be pursued. Under Reagan, an arms boom has provided conditions for growth in this sector in Canada. Although unionists have discussed the idea of converting the arms industry to socially useful production, there have been few concrete achievements. This is not because of the lack of technical expertise, but rather because as long as those who own and control economic life continue to be able to pursue profitable outlets with little control, conversion will remain unlikely. An economy designed for peaceful ends can only be brought about by challenging the basic prerogatives and traditional power of the private sector.

A feminist critique of militarism points out that male power and traditional male values are deeply rooted in our social structure and in the connections between patriarchy and the arms race. Challenging the arms race in isolation from its underlying values and assumptions may lead to short-term victories perhaps, but the structure of power, hierarchy, and domination will remain. A society that actively opposes violence, that stands against degradation, and for equality between men and women, and moves towards an elimination of hierarchy will be less likely to be dominated by values that lead to war preparation and military solutions to conflict. The basic argument is that Canada's contribution to the arms race is not an aberration, or some kind of isolated "bad" policy, but is part of the wider relations of power and domination: U.S. control over Canada, private capital's shaping of the economy, and the wide ideology and practice of patriarchy.

The implications of this analysis are both difficult and challenging. Difficult because we have to confront powerlessness and frustration when we realize what we are up against. Small victories, both necessary and worth fighting for, are difficult enough to achieve, but we must recognize the necessities of a long-term vision and program. While taking on specific aspects of Canada's contribution to the arms race, we must also engage in public debate and discussion of the wider issues of power, popular control over various policies, and democracy. Only the peace and other social movements will raise these questions. If they are avoided, the peace movement will end up only reacting to each government's contribution to the escalation of the arms race without a positive, alternative program of its own.

Finally, we come to the means available for change. The relations of power in society are reflected in state power. It cannot be assumed that the Canadian state is neutral, and outside of the basic social dynamic. Although limited reform is possible, it will only be as a result of large-scale mobilization, and even then the changes will be shaped in such a way as to interfere as little as possible with the fundamental relations of power. For more substantial and long-lasting change it is necessary to shift the basic values, understanding, and concerns at the base of society. Building strong, locally based groups that involve many people from all walks of life is the only way forward. Only a wide sense of vision and involvement at the base of the society will work as a means of directing—or shaking up, perhaps—leadership of the country and challenging the relations of power that shape the arms race.

Notes

1. For a background study of the relationship between U.S. foreign policy and Canadian economic interests, see Victor Levant, *Quiet Complicity: Canadian Involvement in the Vietnam War* (Toronto, 1986).

2. Jan Williams, "Pour un Atlantique du Nord dénucléarisé: le Réseau de l'Atlantique du Nord—Alliance Alternative," in *revue internationale d'action communautaire*, 12/52, Automne 1984.

Part One

An International Perspective on the Peace Movement

Canada, the United States, and the Western Alliance

Major-General (ret.) Leonard Johnson

WHATEVER MIGHT BE SAID in favour of military preparedness, and whether or not it has prevented war in Europe for 40 years, as some contend, it has not achieved the political reconciliation that alone can bring a durable peace. Those who are concerned about this failure blame the politicians for lack of political initiative. But perhaps military preparedness itself, with its self-interested bureaucracies, is making reconciliation impossible.

Perhaps reciprocal fear, the accumulations of durable myths, worst case assumptions, threat exaggerations, institutional ambitions, and the vanities of ambitious people are insurmountable obstacles to peace. Perhaps this would be tolerable, were it benign; but it is not. The dominance of military preparedness over politics leads to militarism, to attempts to solve political problems with military science and technology, to sacrifice of economic and social well-being, and to making more likely the war it seeks to prevent.

"The immediate cause of World War III is the military preparation of it," wrote C. Wright Mills in 1958. Although World War III turned out to be less imminent than Mills thought, it has not been made less likely by developments since 1958. Instead, the necessary conditions for war have been further developed and refined as strategy and technology lead inexorably towards nuclear war. While the preparations continue, politicians, generals, defence bureaucrats, and the public delude themselves that nuclear war, being irrational, is therefore impossible. All that need be done to prevent it is to continue to prepare for it at ever-increasing expense.

In Canada, faith in military preparedness is expressed in dedication to the U.S.-led North Atlantic Alliance as presumed guarantor of Canada's national security. Assumptions of dependency, such as this one, lead to voluntary relinquishment of independence and foreclose alternatives that could better serve the interests of Canada and the alliance.

The companion assumption of the preceding one is that Canada is a military protectorate of the United States, unable or unwilling to pay the costs of its own defence. I am going to argue that both of these assumptions are false, that they are leading to the squandering of defence resources on an irrelevant contribution to the defence of Western Europe, that they are causing legitimate defensive needs to be neglected, and that the presumed necessity for loyalty to U.S. policies prevents the democratic assertiveness on which collective security ultimately depends.

The Assumptions

Any examination of Canadian defence policy must begin with the assumptions that govern it.

An extreme but nevertheless widely held perception of Canada's strategic dependency was expressed by Professor Nils Orvik of the Queen's University Centre for International Relations in an article called "A Defence Doctrine for Canada", published in *Orbis* in 1983. The key premises of his argument were contained in two paragraphs:

> We start with an observation that seems obvious but that nevertheless must be the basis for all discussions on Canadian defence and national security: Canada cannot be effectively defended by its own armed forces. Even if Canadian military units were many times larger than they are now, they would be incapable of defending all parts of the nation against a major threat.

> Canada lacks the military forces it would need in order to guarantee the security of the national territory against a major adversary, and this fact leads us to what may be the most fundamental criterion of a defence doctrine: In the foreseeable future, Canada's national security will depend on military cooperation with the United States and other nations whose national interests and basic values are compatible with Canada's and whose military capabilities are large enough to cover Canada's security needs in addition to their own.

In contradiction to this stands the view expressed in the 1984-85 Estimates of the Department of National Defence:

> One of the features of Canada's geographic and strategic situation is that it is virtually impossible to demonstrate convincingly that Canada's national security against threats of military attack is diminished by reducing the size and capability of the Canadian Forces or is increased by increasing them.

This says there are no military threats to Canada that justify armed forces, implying that the Canadian Forces could safely be abolished. Nothing is said about surveillance and control of airspace, ocean approaches, and territory, or about Prime Minister Mackenzie King's 1938 undertaking not to permit Canada to be used as an avenue of attack on the United States. The statement continues:

> What can be demonstrated, however, is that reductions in the size and capability of the Canadian Forces do subtract from the military capabilities of the collective defence system which has been chosen to preserve Canada's national security. Similarly, it is demonstrable that increases in the size and capabilities of Canada's forces do add to the military capabilities of that collective defence system.

Having said that the marginal effects of changes to Canada's token commitment to NATO are demonstrable, the Department fails to so demonstrate.

Canada's Geostrategic Position

Except for its location between nuclear-armed superpowers threatening to destroy each other, Canada enjoys an enviable geostrategic position. No potentially hostile powers, including the USSR, have the military capability to invade and occupy a country so large, so impenetrable by land, and so remote. As long as the United States remains friendly, Canada will be free from the threat of invasion.

Although the North Atlantic Treaty commits signatories to come to the aid of each other if attacked, there are no contingency plans to deploy European forces in Canada, nor is the need for them foreseen. While Canada's naval forces would likely operate under NATO command in wartime, co-operation could as easily be achieved bilaterally. Thus, NATO is not essential to the defence of North America. Moreover, except for nuclear attack, against which there is no defence in any case, Canada could defend itself without U.S. assistance.

Canada is under no Treaty obligation to maintain forces in Europe. Its 5,400-person contingent, the remnants of forces deployed before Europe rearmed, is a voluntary contribution to the defence of Western Europe. Too small by far to be militarily significant, its attributed cost alone nevertheless exceeds $1 billion per year, more than the budgets of most government departments and agencies. Canada spends more on its unneeded contribution to European defence than it does on the CBC or the marine transportation program, for example. Furthermore, the attributed costs do not include services provided by National Defence Headquarters and other Canadian Forces commands, such as recruiting, training, administration, airlift support, common logistics, reserves, wartime augmentation, and defence of the sea lanes. Perhaps as much as half of all defence expenditures is in some way attributable to the defence of Western Europe.

It is often asserted that this contribution is the price of admittance to membership in NATO councils and various arms control and disarmament forums. This proposition is also false: Canada is part of the NATO region, and the defence of Canada is also the defence of NATO. The Canadian concern, however, has been the defence not of Canada but of Europe.

Opportunity Costs

The real cost of any activity is the foregone opportunity to use the resources for other purposes, whether in other defence tasks or for civilian programs. Northern sovereignty, CBC regional programming, wildlife conservation projects, fisheries improvement, education, youth employment programs, regional development, search and rescue, economic investment, and reduced government deficits are all opportunity costs of Canada's contribution to the defence of Western Europe.

Not least of the opportunity costs are national defence requirements that cannot be met within existing and prospective resource allocations. These include an ice-capable navy with modern warships, replacements for Sea King shipborne helicopters and Tracker aircraft for coastal surveillance and protection, enhanced coastal search and rescue capabilities, logistics and combat support improvements for mobile forces, and—depending on aerospace threat improvements as Star Wars unfolds—augmented development of Northern warning and surveillance capabilities. When defence costs are rising as steeply as they are, it is clearly necessary to allot scarce resources to primary needs and not to discretionary commitments of marginal value.

A Stable Standoff in Europe

It is inconceivable that either European alliance—NATO or the Warsaw Treaty Organization—would deliberately attack the other. The uncertainties and probable consequences of conflict between the nuclear-armed superpowers are too awesome for either of them to risk for any conceivable potential gain.

Accordingly, in the absence of a political settlement in Europe leading to disarmament, it is likely that a standoff will prevail there as long as the superpowers are engaged in their hegemonial domains and as long as Germany remains divided. This standoff is robust, stable, and tolerant of marginal change in the balance of military forces. Canada's forces in Europe, even if quadrupled, would not increase its own security or that of its allies, nor would it be diminished if Canada withdrew from the alliance altogether.

Canada's Political Aims

In or out of NATO, Canada's paramount aim must be to prevent nuclear war. Canada should also promote political reconciliation in Europe, leading in time to the withdrawal of all foreign forces, to substantial disarmament, and to the progressive abandonment of NATO and the Warsaw Treaty Organization. These objectives can be achieved only if the superpowers are first persuaded to stop preparing for nuclear war and to abandon aggressive, threatening, and self-destructive policies in favour of detente. If there is to be peace and security in Europe, or anywhere else, the superpowers and their allies must assert the primacy of politics over military confrontation in their relations.

The likelihood of nuclear war is being increased by nuclear war-fighting strategies and weapons capable of attacks against nuclear retaliatory capabilities. Stable mutual deterrence is giving way to preparations to fight nuclear wars. Weapons technology is deepening global insecurity. And the nuclear arms race, not the underlying political causes that purportedly justify it, is the paramount threat. Preparations for nuclear war, condemned by the churches as immoral, by international lawyers as illegal, and by philosophers as irrational, are only making nuclear war more likely.

The Crisis of Western Leadership

Since 1980 the risk of war has been increased by the ideological rigidity and militant anti-communism of the interventionist Reagan administration. One of the manifestations of this is the military intervention in Central America, where the United States has become the aggressor and chief obstacle to the Contadora peace process. This aggression is not justified by any objective threat to U.S. security; it is not supported within the Western alliance; it is inimical to Western interests and to those of the United States itself; it is corroding the moral authority of Western leadership, and it is giving the Soviet Union another opportunity to become involved in the Western Hemisphere. As a threat to the unity and cohesion of NATO, it is a threat to the alliance itself.

The authors of the militarist policies that are having such disastrous results are a small elite of U.S. citizens who gained control over their country's foreign policy in 1950, at a critical time in history. This group, known as the Committee on the Present Danger, disbanded after the Vietnam War but re-formed with some of its original members in 1976 to oppose the SALT II agreement.

With the help of the late Senator Joseph R. McCarthy and his political terrorism, the effects of which continue, the Committee has seen to the triumph of mindless ideology over reason in U.S. foreign policy. The Committee's work led to war and defeat in Vietnam and to the deaths of millions in Asia and Central America; it has created the greatest apparatus of death in human history; it has cowed liberal intellectuals, the Congress, the bureaucracy, and all Presidents since Truman, and it has now gained power in the United States. The military-industrial complex that President Eisenhower warned about in his farewell address on January 20, 1961, is now running the United States without effective opposition. U.S. leadership has been corrupted and destroyed with the capital and moral stock of a once-great democracy.

Failure to oppose U.S. militarist policies is to acquiesce and become complicit. The time has come for the leaders of the Western alliance to oppose the actions of their superpower champion, because unity at all costs cannot be an end in itself. In the long run, the alliance can be effective and worth keeping only if it stands for something worthwhile, and only if it is willing to uphold the principles its people profess. To consent to preparations for nuclear war and to U.S. aggression in Central America is to make shallow pretense of democracy, human rights, and justice.

In the absence of effective domestic opposition in the United States, it is incumbent on the leaders of the Western alliance to provide loyal opposition to policies threatening collective security and which are legally, morally, and ethically repugnant to their peoples. Their vital tasks are to curb the containment militarism that has been U.S. policy since 1950, to stop U.S. intervention in Central America, and to build a just and durable peace.

As a neighbour and ally of the United States, Canada has a particular obligation to act. Moreover, because Canada is less dependent on the United States for its military security than the Europeans profess to be, this country can act freely without jeopardizing any U.S. security guarantee. Bold and courageous political action, commanding support everywhere including the United States, would be an infinitely more valuable contribution to collective security than a symbolic contribution to the defence of Western Europe.

Canada's Defence Options

Far from being a military dependency, as Professor Orvik asserts, Canada enjoys an unusual degree of immunity from military attack and commensurate discretion in its defence activities. Apart from direct protection of the country against minor threats and those tasks needed to assure the United States against surprise attack from the North, there are no strong claims for defence resources. There is no compelling reason why Canada should continue to contribute to the defence of Western Europe, an economic and military superpower, nor, for that matter, are there any legal, moral, or military reasons why Canadians should prepare to fight in foreign wars.

What is important is that Canada and its allies help to tame the Reagan administration, exorcise the ghost of McCarthy, and eradicate the right-wing ideology that is destroying the United States and making it such a threat to humankind.

The Empire Strikes Back – Reflections on the Arms Race

Bryan Palmer

Spurning the clouds written with curses,
stamps the stony law to dust,
loosing the eternal horses from
the dens of night, crying:
　　EMPIRE IS NO MORE! AND NOW THE
　　LION AND THE WOLF SHALL CEASE.
　　　　—Willam Blake (1793)

History, Stephen said, is a nightmare
from which I am trying to awake.
　　　　—James Joyce (1922)

IT IS NOW IMPOSSIBLE to ignore the arms race and the popular expressions of discontent that are mounted daily against it. Each week's news carries the message into the public arena. Demonstrations in the West routinely draw hundreds of thousands, while in the East it is becoming more difficult to muffle the voices of resistance to militarism in the nuclear age. Riotous antinuclear street confrontations erupt in West Germany, while women's survival camps offer a more orderly and persistent opposition in England, on the continent, and in regions of North America. All the while, the theatre of negotiation between the superpowers continues, as it has since 1945: Here authority, poker-faced, trades insults and rhetorical denunciations, as well as the odd option or offer of reduction, seemingly unconcerned with the catastrophic implications of a misplayed hand. The media is finally attentive. This is a consequence, not of coverage, but of action. The self-activity of masses of protesters opposed to the nuclear nightmare has created a context in which nuclear weapons and their detractors cannot be shunted to the periphery. It has even moved the hands of the White House and the Kremlin, structuring their language, if not their intentions, in the direction of disarmament: We hear, for the first time in years, of zero options and deep cuts, cynically orchestrated to secure a phantom advantage or to score a propaganda point.

Indeed, so pressing are the threats of the nuclear age that they have even entered into the discourse of history, a discipline which in Canada is often reluctant to step out of the past to confront the present. A relatively new text on twentieth-century Canada authored by a central committee of professional historians composed of J.L. Granatstein, Irving Abella, David J. Bercuson, R. Craig Brown, and H. Blair Neatby closes with words of worry:

> Above all, there is the ominous and ever present nuclear balance of terror. This is one area that is definitely not in Ottawa's hands, one problem that can be settled only in Moscow and Washington. Few, in the early 1980s, feel any confidence in their ability to find a workable solution. The regime in Moscow has been talking tough and pushing its hard line in Afghanistan and in Poland, employing its Cuban surrogates in East Africa and Angola, and waiting uneasily for Chairman Andropov to put his own imprint on the state. In Washington President Reagan's simplistic solutions to complicated problems seem increasingly facile, although Washington's escalating defence budgets and tough talk make many Americans—and many Canadians—uneasy.[1]

What is significant here is how the nuclear threat is presented.

First, there is the insistence that the arms race can be halted only in Washington and Moscow. True on one level, this pragmatic deference to the state and the institutions of international relations sidesteps the whole issue of popular initiatives. Second, in its cavalier and ahistorical presentation of the current crisis, we are left with a distinct impression of imbalance within the threatening "balance of terror". Things seem to have happened since 1979, and in a curious way. Whereas America's warmaking is personalized as a consequence of Ronald Reagan's extremism (no coincidence among historians whose work consistently trivializes the state by equating it with an individualistic wielding of power), the Soviets—a "regime"—are following a much more structured path of tough-minded, heavy-handed policy. One wonders at this. For every Afghanistan there is surely an equally bloody Turkey, the carnage in

Poland is not yet piled as viciously high as that of El Salvador, and sur-
rogates have done their work as surreptitiously in Chile, South Africa, and
Israel as in the Horn of Africa or Angola. But we hear only the sound of
one hand clapping. What is missing in this liberal conclusion is any sense
of the historical origins of the arms race, of its reciprocal character, and of
what it is that will stop the apparent drift to war.

These are large gaps, and should be filled in as part of any reflection
on the arms race. They are serious deficiencies, for they pervade thinking
on disarmament and have become the stock in trade, not only of liberal
critics,[2] but also of radical opponents of nuclear weapons[3] and of conservative defenders of deterrence.[4] They form the convoluted substance of
former Prime Minister Pierre Trudeau's 1983 "Open Letter" on the testing
of Cruise missiles in Canada. The "Open Letter" provides a concise statement of the approaches to defence of successive Canadian governments,
before and since. In that document we have six essential points:

1. the dichotomous politics of "our freedom" and "Soviet
   totalitarianism";
2. under totalitarianism no dissent is possible and the Soviet peoples cannot voice their protests;
3. Western peace movements "have remained relatively silent about the in-
   stallation" of Soviet SS-20s in Europe;
4. American deployment of Cruise and Pershing missiles aims to "protect
   Europe";
5. the Soviet Union is the aggressor in the arms race;
6. the Canadian policy of suffocation was rejected by the USSR,
   necessitating Canada's alliance with the North Atlantic Treaty
   Organization's two-track strategy of (a) negotiating the removal of
   Soviet SS-20 missiles; and (b) preparing to deploy Cruise and Pershing
   II missiles so as to strengthen the NATO alliance's bargaining hand and
   pressure the Russians in the direction of serious negotiations.[5]

Pierre Trudeau's "Open Letter", not unlike the statement by the five
historians of twentieth-century Canada, is a product of the post-war years,
a position written out of the very Cold War context that has led from the
nuclear blackmail of the East by the West in the 1950s, into a reluctant
detente in the 1963-76 years, towards the revival of the Cold War and the
escalation of the arms race in the last decade.

Trudeau's self-serving posturing on "freedom" and "totalitarianism" (like the historians' more benign distinction between policy and
personality: *theirs* is a system, *ours* is an elective democracy) is nothing less
than the reproduction of the categories of the Cold War. Such rigid pigeon-
holing has frozen West and East in blocs, both analytic and diplomatic.
Such a freeze blinds many—left, right, and centre—to the presence and

potential of the autonomous peace groups of the East, and Trudeau's denial of their existence is, interpreted charitably, but the official voice of a public kept uninformed by Cold War misunderstanding and media blackout.[6] His attack on the Western peace movement's relative silence on Soviet arms cannot be assessed so moderately. It is a lie, a toned-down variant of those now-deflated claims made only recently that the peace movement was a Russian front.[7] For the Western peace movements *have* opposed Soviet arms, consistently and sensibly. In Europe, European Nuclear Disarmament's most famous early slogan was, "No Cruise, No SS-20s",[8] and rallies in North America, while understandably aiming their sights most directly at such weapons as the Trident, the Pershing II, or the Cruise, have not avoided Russian responsibilities in the arms race. To think, moreover, that we must speak for Europe (where the SS-20s are sited and aimed, for they cannot reach North America) is to adopt the same bloc mentality that the Cold War thrives upon—that America and Russia are locked into irreconcilable antagonisms, around which the rest of the world must polarize for protection. But Europe has already spoken to this question. It finds little security in missile deployments, from its east or its west, and can harbour no gratification in the knowledge that both superpowers may well be content to fight World War III on European soil.[9] Trudeau's assertion that Cruise and Pershing II missiles "protect" Europe is thus a blatant reversal of realities: These are menacing rather than defensive developments and are challenged by those who perceive them in this light.

The two final claims of this "Open Letter"—that the Soviets are the aggressors and that Canada, while committed to suffocation of the arms race, is necessarily forced, through Russian actions, to accept NATO strategy—are no less a product of Cold War thought and action, and no less untenable. For to appreciate the extent to which Trudeau's letter has been conditioned by the post-war climate of the Cold War, we must turn where our historians did not: to history, the origins and consequences of more than three decades of Soviet-American relations, shifting balances of international power, and militaristic innovation. There in that past, among the complex consequences, were formed ideologies and material structures (economic and technological) that together have proven decisive in the current making of World War III.

The Return of the Cold War

The Cold War precedes the arms race, which after all is only its most potentially destructive subset. Although assuming its most vitriolic form in the post-Yalta period, the Cold War has in fact existed since 1917, as

William Appleman Williams long ago argued.[10] Since the Bolshevik Revolution, with the East supposedly committed to proletarian revolution around the world, the West has striven to contain the spread of supposedly Soviet-inspired and -supported insurrection. Premised upon mutual hostilities that have hardened and become locked in place, the Cold War has outlived the regimes that have nourished it, regimes that now bear little resemblance to their ancestors of six decades past. Less and less an expression of *realpolitik* (if it ever was that to begin with), the Cold War is, as E.P. Thompson suggests, more and more a self-reproducing, deeply reciprocal order of immense value to those whose wielding of power, in East and West, is shored up by the threat from the Other, be that other aggressive totalitarian communism, ever on the prowl for another nation-state victim, or capitalistic imperialism, driven by an inexorable logic to consume the resources of the Third World and curb the power and potential of the socialist Second.[11]

But for all of its continuity, the Cold War has been characterized by marked fluctuations. In the post-World War II years, these movements provide a scale upon which it is possible to weigh the nuclear balance of terror, a course in which to situate the arms race itself.[12] Four clear periods emerge in this overview.

Immediately after World War II, with the promise of an "American Century" looming large in U.S. foreign policy objectives, and anti-Sovietism sinking its roots in the State Department (where the Committee on the Present Danger was forged) the Cold War crystallized in an East-West ideological freeze. In the years to follow, this freeze overtook vast regions of what, during World War II, had appeared to be ground of guarded mutual understanding and reluctant agreement. A temporary thaw of cautious compromise, evident as late as 1945, quickly retreated to a barren glacial-like terrain, upon which East and West secured their footing the better to dislodge their adversary. In this consolidation of the Cold War, initiatives were seized by the United States and replicated by the Soviet Union: The explosion of the atom and hydrogen bombs, the forging of bloc alliances, and the stockpiling of nuclear weapons were all developments of these years. They did not lead inevitably to a vigorous arms race, however, for there was no effective race being run. The Soviets were lapped, not once, but many times, and as Roy and Zhores Medvedev have argued, Russia was persistently intimidated by superior American technology, which was often publicly displayed to embarrass communist leaders. (And, given the ossification so prominent in a bureaucratized Soviet politics, those leaders of 1955-62—Gromyko, Brezhnev, Ustinov, Andropov—remained at the centre of political power well into the late 1970s and early 1980s. They no doubt retained memories of past indignities, such as the U-2 surveillance flights that were used to disrupt May Day celebrations on Red Square.)[13] Thus much of the Eisenhower years saw little in the way of increases in U.S. defence spending, nor did they witness an escalation in militaristic interventions around the world on the part of either the United States or the Soviet Union. The former was perhaps relatively smug in its superiority, the latter somewhat cowed by a belligerent United States that was more than a match for a Soviet Union scarred deeply by World War II and yet to catch its second wind in the Sputnik era.

This state of U.S. arrogance and Soviet paranoia was destined to propel both powers into an arms race of previously unanticipated dimensions. The starter's pistol rang out in the late 1950s, and between 1957 and 1962 the runners were constantly jockeying for position. By the time of the Cuban missile crisis, both competitors had come close to fouling out.

Eisenhower's New Look came under hawkish attack in 1957 with the secretive and irresponsible "Gaither Report" (*Deterrence and Survival in the Nuclear Age*) and Henry Kissinger's *Nuclear Weapons and Foreign Policy*, a key document in the debasement of diplomacy, with its veiled endorsement of "planned" and "limited" nuclear wars. Under the reign of Camelot, Kennedy increased the defence budget a hefty 15 per cent in one year, and old Cold War warriors such as former Committee on the Present Danger member Paul Nitze were called into the State and Defence departments to advise the new administration on Soviet advances in arms production.

To be sure, the Soviets too were marching forward, consolidating the Warsaw Pact (1955), crushing rebel forces in Hungary (1956), developing ICBMs (1957), shooting down Gary Powers's U-2 with the first sophisticated Soviet anti-aircraft missiles (1960), and moving a part of their nuclear arsenal dangerously close to the United States (1962). The Soviets were now in the race, determined, in Nikita Khrushchev's words, to show the United States that "they couldn't hide behind their technology forever".[14] Out of all this came the shrill cry of Soviet expansionism and the hysteria of the "missile gap", a complete fabrication that depicted America being overtaken by Russia in the arms race.

The "American Century", so confidently proclaimed at the end of World War II, had lasted barely a decade. The empires—East and West—were striking back. The United States, for its part, risked the most, aggressively aware that in reality it held a series of upper hands, the nuclear not the least of them. Within two brief years the Kennedy administration faced more international crises—Berlin, Southeast Asia, and Cuba among them—than the Eisenhower presidency had confronted in its entire eight-year duration.[15]

The Cuban crisis was the most explosive of these, and saw the United States successfully call the Soviet nuclear bluff. But plenty of chips remained on the table—more than enough to keep both parties in the game. By 1965-66, the Soviets secured, for the first time, the capability to reach the continental United States with nuclear weapons. Between 1966 and 1968, the USSR undertook an accelerated buildup of strategic missiles, launched its initial ballistic-missile armed submarines, and developed arms powered by solid fuel. (In all of those realms the original advances had been registered by the United States in 1960-61.)[16]

As early as 1963, signs emerged that both empires recognized the new context of the mid-1960s: The destructive capacity of the United States and the developing arsenal of the Soviet Union ensured that a nuclear confrontation would be a war without winners. To engage in such a war would be to court Mutually Assured Destruction (MAD). This entailed certain agreed-upon procedures: arms buildup for purposes of deterrence, detente, peaceful coexistence, and eventually strategic arms limitation talks. Indeed, under Nixon, expenditures on national defence as a percentage of Gross National Product declined from almost 9 per cent in the late 1960s to less than 5.5 per cent in the early 1970s, and military interventions around the world declined in comparison to the presidencies of Kennedy and Johnson. Deterrence seemed to be working: The Cold War thaw of 1963-76 eased the tensions associated with the arms race.[17]

But deterrence contained a fatal flaw. The relaxation of Cold War tensions had not, of course, stopped the arms race, for a fundamental, if contradictory, premise of the period of detente was that deterrence rested on the fear of MAD, which required the willingness to use weapons, the need to develop overkill capacity, and the ongoing refinement of nuclear arms.[18] An irrational process had apparently given birth to a rational relationship.

Soviet leaders, as Marxists, should have foreseen the instabilities inherent in this fragile balance of detente. For the United States had no planned economy. Overlapping realms of the defence and industrial sectors—aerospace and electrical components, for instance—came to rely upon deterrence spending to provide the profit margins that obscured the general economic slide towards stagnation in the late 1970s.

Compared to the flush years of the 1950s and 1960s, when prosperity and world dominance seemed the peculiar preserve of an entrenched U.S. hegemony, the 1970s proved to be a decade of unambiguous decline. Average annual rates of growth for real wages and productivity plummeted by 100 per cent, while the pace of inflation accelerated to as much as three times its previous level. Unemployment climbed at the same time that the rate of profit and investment dipped. Capital continued its flight to Europe, the Pacific Rim, and the Third World, where wages were lower and returns on capital higher; Japanese capitalists began to overtake their American counterparts. In this context of pervasive and worsening recession, entire sectors of the U.S. economy took refuge behind the high profits, cost overruns, inefficiency, and security of militarist contracts, many of them nuclear-related. Detente was a luxury that U.S. capitalism in decline could no longer afford.[19]

By the beginning of the 1980s such corporate spheres were being sustained by military orders. Boeing's drop in demand for commercial jets was offset by contracts for Cruise missiles, helicopters, and bombers; Chrysler was bailed out of bankruptcy by the U.S. Army, now its largest customer; McDonnell Douglas built planes for both the Air Force and the Navy. Corporate stock prices for the "electronic warfare group" jumped 100 per cent in price, and "defence issues" generally advanced by 50 per cent. Defence Secretary Caspar Weinberger proclaimed that arms buildup was a vital part of the administration's program to "revitalize America". In the pages of financial journals the headlines were ecstatic: "Congress Goes Wild on Defence Spending" and "Happy Days are Here Again for Arms Makers." By the end of 1980, in actual, if not acknowledged, dollars, the U.S. military budget comprised 9.5 per cent of the GNP (78 per cent higher than official figures implied).[20]

This turn to an economistic militarism, so structured in the direction of sophisticated and innovative high technology, was buttressed by shifts in foreign policy. After the defeat in Vietnam, and during the final relaxed years of detente (1972-77), great pressures were exerted, by the public and by the State Department officials, to avoid adventuristic involvement in Third World struggles that many perceived could not be suppressed or intimidated. A "Vietnam Syndrome" caught hold of the general population, and even given the reduction in government monies allocated to defence in this period, 72 per cent of those polled in the mid-1970s thought it overfunded.[21] As the first step in overcoming this "Vietnam Syndrome", the American advocates of defence turned decisively towards the nuclear option, and once more beat the panic drums of a Soviet arms buildup. On Veteran's Day, 1976, the old Committee on the Present Danger reconstituted itself and, led by Paul Nitze and Richard Pipes, began an assault on the "soft" relations with the Russians that had prevailed since 1963. This group and those around it, originally marginalized by Carter, then accepted by him, and later highly influential in the Reagan administration, articulated the strategic and ideological direction of the 1980s: nuclear war as possibility, assault on the "Vietnam

Syndrome'' and increasing intervention in the Third World, and, finally, the return to a relentless denigration of the Soviet Union, again persistently deplored as totalitarian, expansionist, and mendacious.[22]

Carter, originally committed publicly to the reduction of military spending, was increasing it by 1978. Long before the Soviet invasion of Afghanistan and well before the Polish rebellion (both of which, along with the suppression of ethnic minorities and dissidents in the USSR, simply loaded up an already pointed American ideological gun), a sustained arms buildup in the United States was underway, drawing an appropriate Soviet response. SS-20s and new U.S. missile deployments in Europe followed, rather than led, such developments, and the crises of 1979 were preceded by the collapse of the second round of the Strategic Arms Limitation Talks and U.S. presidential directives that went beyond notions of peaceful coexistence. With the oil crisis of 1973-74 fresh in the collective memory of Americans, both bourgeois and proletarian, Carter asserted that the United States would now walk loudly and carry a big stick into those spheres of interest threatened by the USSR. If necessary, war would be waged to secure the economic health of the ''free world''. Under Reagan this beginning was given new teeth. Between 1981 and 1985, estimated militaristic expenditure was expected to total some $1.5 trillion, surpassing the momentum of the original Cold War (1950-54). America is ''rearming''.

We are thus treated to the return of the Cold War. And the arms race is run with a new recklessness and moral abandon, fuelled by economistic and ideological imperatives, but driven by unprecedented technological determinations as relatively autonomous and as awesomely threatening as any previously known to humankind. The age of MAD, grinding to a halt in the late 1970s, has given way to the ''Nuclear Use Tactics'' of the 1980s. Technological refinements have ushered us into an epoch of NUTS.[23]

Star (and Other) Wars

The arms race has now been running for more than a quarter of a century. Both superpowers possess sufficient quantities of nuclear weapons to kill the entire population of the world many times over.[24] They have had this overabundance of weaponry, this overkill, for decades. So it is not quantities that threaten to push us over the abyss—at least not quantities alone. Rather, it is the qualitative transformation of the technology of nuclear weapons that has revolutionized the arms race. Related explicitly to the economistic militarism of an America in decline, dependent upon the certainty of returns to nuclear technology's ubiquitous research, innovation, and overproduction, the "modernization" of nuclear weaponry has played a significant role in revamping U.S. strategic objectives, convincing many that the rearmed empire now has the first-strike capability that will allow it to fight and win a nuclear war.[25]

For the time being, the "gains" recorded in this new arms race have been, as they were in the past, decidedly one-sided, resting almost solely with the United States. But the Soviet Union, if the past can be relied upon to indicate the direction of future developments, will not be far behind in registering its own "gains".

Four major developments have occurred in the recent past,[26] all of which enhance the first-strike capability of the United States and force the more backward, but still powerfully equipped, Soviet Union into a corner of greater and greater expenditure, where a quick retaliation may seem the only plausible response:

1. New systems of missile delivery and multiple-launching such as the Cruise and MX (allocated $1.5 billion in research money under Carter's 1980 budget and later the subject of much controversy given Reagan's attempts to increase the defence budget) have now redefined the nature of nuclear warfare because of their accuracy and increased destructive potential: Estimates in certain circles in the United States are that Soviet land-based missiles (70-80 per cent of the USSR's nuclear stockpile) could be targeted and hit with one shot 92 per cent of the time.
2. More sophisticated defence systems, in the form of antiballistic missiles and submarine technology (16 per cent of the U.S. naval budget is currently devoted to the latter) have cultivated the view that the United States could defend itself adequately against nuclear attack.
3. The development of more effective nuclear submarines such as the Trident has led the United States to mount roughly 60 per cent of its nuclear arsenal on highly mobile and difficult-to-locate seafaring vessels, thereby upgrading its defences against attack at the same time that it improves its capability to launch a first-strike.
4. The potential use of high-intensity laser beams, travelling a mile in the same time that it takes a missile to travel a solitary inch, enables the United States to hit Soviet missiles before they are even out of their silos.

The Reagan-Weinberger Strategic Defense Initiative, aimed at developing laser and particle-beam weapons, adds a new dimension to this final realm. Claiming that the refinement and perfection of such a defence system would enable the United States to destroy Soviet missiles in flight, thereby rendering the USSR arsenal "impotent and obsolete", Reagan's objectives are noteworthy because they depart from three decades of strategy that has regarded massive retaliation to a nuclear strike as the appropriate deterring response. The Soviets have denounced the proposals as "bellicose", "insane", and "irresponsible", while Democrats in the Senate have castigated "the reckless Star Wars schemes of the President".[27]

Such technologies, where developed, are of course untested in the actual conditions of battle, and are subject to a diverse range of error, both human and mechanical.[28] Under differing climatic conditions, they may well prove far less capable than their advocates in competing sectors of the military-industrial complex promise they will be. Of this much we can be sure. But these innovations are nevertheless inherently destabilizing, for there are those who believe in them and what they are told about them. They push the promise of a new "American Century", defended by weapons and defence systems that will enable the United States to "prevail".

Leading figures in this Strangelovian "Holocaust Lobby" include Edward Teller (the Hungarian-born physicist and Soviet basher who created the H-bomb); pioneer nuclear-use theorist Paul Nitze; his Committee on the Present Danger comrade, Richard Pipes (of Harvard's Russian Research Center); and the boy-wonder of defence analysts, Richard Perle.[29] These men, and others like them, are captivated by the promise of a United States that is claiming the ability to place laser weapons on the moon.

Human and technological ingenuity of this order, capable of creating weapons that E.P. Thompson has remarked will be, literally, lunatic, has convinced many in policy posts that the United States should move from MAD to NUTS, taking the empires' wars off the planet and into the galaxy. The possibility, if not the practice, of technological innovation impels us towards World War III.

The Force Within: The Role of the Canadian State

All of this should lay to rest the oft-repeated claim that the Soviets are aggressors in the arms race. Every significant technological innovation has, historically, been pioneered by the United States, just as more recently each upping of the strategic ante has come from the United States. The Cruise missile was in the planning stage well in advance of the deployment of the Soviet SS-20s, while SALT II went unratified long before the much condemned USSR interventions in Afghanistan and Poland. It is the reactive character of the arms race, the reciprocality of the Cold War, that stands out, rather than some judgemental categorization of blame.

What, then, is the role of the Canadian state in this area? How has Canada functioned as a national entity in the world affairs of the nuclear age? Is it, for instance, simply a matter of individuals—Mulroney, Trudeau, or Pearson—deciding what to do and, as Walter Gordon has argued, changing their minds for the worse on the issue of nuclear weapons?[30] We must resist such personalization of the state. The Canadian state is not some lottery up for grabs by any winner who then exercises the voluntarism of his own choosing. It is, like the arms race itself, far more of a process than a piece of property, and it is structured so as to draw to its pinnacle those capable of adapting to its needs rather than challenging them. While not impervious to pressures from outside, it is extremely unlikely that it will reform itself internally.

To understand this we must turn, once again, to history, one part of which is obviously economic subordination to a world power on our doorstep, another part—political subservience to the foreign policy objectives of that power—a subservience more complicated and nuanced than simple acquiescence. For there are, buried deeply in the ashes of Canada's recent past, remnants of attempts to establish some semblance of independence in foreign policy.

The inter-war years saw frustrated efforts to chart a course of "middle power status" for Canada in which the country's foreign policy would be with the United States but not necessarily of it in every particular. Out of this experience came the unique role that Canada would play in the later evolution of the Cold War and the arms race. Canada was to be a moderating influence upon a great power prone to bellicosity. Its role would be not so much to bend uncomplaining before the winds of U.S. objectives, as it would be to act as a moral weatherman, explaining and rationalizing the inevitable.

By the end of World War II only the illusion of Canada as a "middle power" remained. With the dawn of the nuclear age, and the subdivision of the world by the great powers, Canada fell quickly into step with the international and military objectives of the United States, intent upon picking through the leftovers of the "American Century". It enthusiastically joined in the creation of NATO in 1949, willingly participated in the construction of the Distant Early Warning Line (DEW Line) in the early 1950s, embraced NORAD (North American Air Defence Agreement) in 1957, and signed the Canada-U.S. Defence Sharing Agreement in 1958.

In an age in which we now know the United States to have possessed unquestioned nuclear superiority, Canada became an essential part of U.S. nuclear-armed strength. One aspect of this integration lay in the ease with which Canadian political leaders slipped into the guise of Cold War warriors, with Liberals, Conservatives, and Co-operative Commonwealth

Federationists falling in step with the ideology of the age. External Affairs figure, future Nobel Peace Prize winner, and mid-1960s Liberal Prime Minister Lester B. Pearson articulated the conventional approach to international relations as early as 1948: "The chief menace today is subversive aggressive communism. There are no fireproof houses in the atomic age. Our frontier is wherever free men are struggling against totalitarian tyranny." If these words spoke to specific commitments, another External Affairs minister indicated that attachment to middle power status, however illusory the reality of Canadian autonomy, had its concrete attractions. "The best place to defend Canada," he said, "was as far away from our shores as possible."[31]

In the years to come, this public attachment to the facade of middle-power independence, along with acceptance of Cold War ideology and a virulent anti-Sovietism that fit well with U.S. foreign policy, would march side by side. In the period from 1962 to 1968, the Conservative Diefenbaker government fell over its confused stand on arming Canadian anti-aircraft missiles, while Pearson's Liberals, picking up the political pieces, shifted their antagonism for nuclear weapons, agreed to arm missiles with nuclear warheads, won the election, and then in later years backed away from nuclear arms once again. Canada was to have no nuclear weapons of its own, although it would have U.S. nuclear weapons, engage in vast military trade, and participate in a North Atlantic defence system and the Atlantic alliance.

By the 1980s, with the collapse of whole sectors in the industrial and manufacturing spheres compounded by the decline in oil prices and the glut in natural resource markets, Canadian high-technology production would be of most significance in the arms race and in the more generalized drift towards militarism. It is here, of course, that "arms" for the aerospace industry (as in the recent space shuttle) are developed, guidance systems for the Cruise perfected, and the plastic parts for the nose-cones of the MX contracted. And it is this realm that has benefited most acutely from the institutionalization of Canadian-U.S. military ties·in the form of defence sharing agreements and the political integration of Canada into U.S. foreign policy objectives.

Such background and contemporary development reconcile the apparent contradiction between Liberal Prime Minister Trudeau's 1978 United Nations speech, calling for a suffocation of the arms race, and his 1981 promise to "show the Soviet Union that we can meet them gun for gun if necessary".[32] His "Open Letter" of May 1983, firm in its resolve to test the Cruise and counter Soviet aggression, but pious in its concern for the world's survival in the face of the nuclear arms race, takes on a measure of political coherence. These are not statements of an idiosyncratic and individualistic statesman, grappling with the rough realities of power that most of us cannot comprehend. They are instead the logical outcome of decades of Canadian political economy and diplomacy, in which the Canadian state obscured its essential role in the rhetoric of detachment and high principle in order to speak all the more effectively for essential U.S. priorities. The Canadian political establishment attempts to perpetuate a myth of independence, all the while rationalizing and shoring up U.S. atomic diplomacy.

Canada, in spite of what its rulers say, and however distant we have been historically from the battlefields, is nevertheless an integral part of the arms race that threatens, not just this or that corner of the globe, but the entire world. It *is* a force. Weapons-production sharing agreements link Canada and the United States and, like defence systems, inevitably structure Canadian industrial centres and ports into targeting patterns; U.S. nuclear weapons have, for years, been stored at Comox, British Columbia; and wide-ranging testing, involving not only Cruise missiles but also conventional weapons of value to nuclear-use theorists, takes place across the country from Goose Bay, Newfoundland, to Nanoose Bay, Vancouver Island. Litton Systems Canada Limited and Boeing of Canada are lynchpins in the production of components and guidance systems of the threatening Cruise and MX projects. Litton alone has received over $46-million of public monies in the form of subsidies, grants, and interest-free loans.

In masking the Canadian state's accommodation to U.S. foreign policy needs in the rhetoric and mythology of the independence of a "middle power", politicians have been attempting to perpetuate the legitimation that Canada offers the U.S. empire in the arms race. It is time to turn this around, to step into the breach created by the mythology of a "middle power", and call the Canadian state to order, to create a counter-force of peaceful initiative that will reach beyond the categories of the Cold War.

Not only in Moscow and Washington, then, can the Cold War be challenged and the arms race resisted. Voices that tell us this speak the language of despair, cynicism, and ultimate defeat. For the superpowers have themselves met six thousand times since 1945 to discuss disarmament. Their failures have been legion; their day has passed.[33] The force must pass to new hands, unimpeded by the glacial rigor mortis of the Cold Warriors.

In Europe this has already happened; in Canada it must develop. Then and only then will the cry of the eternal forces of resistance— "Empire is no more"—echo throughout East and West. Then and only then can the world's peoples awake from that historical nightmare that terrorizes East and West in the nuclear age.

Notes

1. J.L. Granatstein et al., *Twentieth-Century Canada* (Toronto, 1983), pp. 432-433.

2. See especially Ernie Regehr and Simon Rosenblum, eds., *Canada and the Nuclear Arms Race* (Toronto, 1983), pp. 191-222.

3. See my "Immobilism and the Peace Movement," *Canadian Dimension* (September 1983).

4. Note the review of Regehr and Rosenblum by a former Canadian Ambassador to NATO and current Distinguished Visiting Professor at Georgetown's Institute for the Study of Diplomacy: John G.H. Halstead, "Nuclear Arms, Nuclear Arguments," *Globe and Mail*, 25 June 1983.

5. The letter was of course widely reproduced, and I have drawn upon "An Open letter from Pierre Trudeau on cruise testing," *Vancouver Sun*, 10 May 1983.

6. On the Eastern peace groups see Adam Hochschild, "The Eastern Front," *Mother Jones* (September-October 1982), pp. 30-37, 52-53; Suzanne Gordon, "From the Other Shore: Movements for Nuclear Disarmament in Eastern Europe," *Working Papers* (March-April 1983), pp. 33-40; Jean Stead and Danielle Grünberg, *Moscow Independent Peace Group* (London, 1982); Ferenc Köszegi and E.P. Thompson, *The New Hungarian Peace Movement* (London, 1982); "The War that Never Ended: Thompson Talks END," *In These Times*, 4-10 May 1983, pp. 12-13.

7. See, for instance, *Vancouver Sun*, 10 December 1981; and *Globe and Mail*, 11 December 1981. The FBI has recently confirmed that there is little Soviet influence in the peace movement in the United States. In Canada, a Royal Canadian Mounted Police (RCMP) agent who infiltrated the peace movement and supposedly played a leading organizational role in Ottawa found no evidence of Soviet control among disarmament groups. See " 'I spied for the RCMP,' peace organizer claims," *Vancouver Province*, 30 June 1983, an article that undercuts Solicitor General Robert Kaplan's claims that the peace movement was not under surveillance.

8. See Mark Abley, "The European Peace Movement," in Regehr and Rosenblum, *Canada and the Nuclear Arms Race*, p. 93.

9. On these and other related points, see the essays by Thompson, Myrdal and Smith in E.P. Thompson and Dan Smith, eds., *Protest and Survive* (Harmondsworth, 1980), pp. 9-61, 75-125.

10. Among other writings: William Appleman Williams, *The Tragedy of American Diplomacy* (New York, 1962).

11. See E.P. Thompson, *Beyond the Cold War: A New Approach to the Arms Race and Nuclear Annihilation* (New York, 1982), pp. 153-188.

12. The following draws upon Alan Wolfe, *The Rise and Fall of the "Soviet Threat": Domestic Sources of the Cold War Consensus* (Washington, 1979), esp. pp. 7-32.

13. Roy Medvedev and Zhores Medvedev, "The USSR and the Arms Race," *New Left Review* 130 (November-December 1981), esp. pp. 10-14.

14. *Khruschev Remembers—The Last Testament* (New York, 1974), pp. 443-453.

15. See Henry Fairlie, *The Kennedy Promise: The Politics of Expectation* (Garden City, 1973).

16. Robert Aldridge, "The Deadly Race: A Look at U.S.-U.S.S.R. Nuclear Capabilities and Intentions," in *Waging Peace: A Handbook for the Struggle to Abolish Nuclear Weapons*, ed. Jim Wallis (San Francisco, 1982), pp. 32.

17. See Paul Joseph, "From MAD to NUTS: The Growing Danger of Nuclear War," *Socialist Review* 61 (January-February 1982), pp. 17-20; Wolfe, *Rise and Fall of the "Soviet Threat"*, pp. 22-25.

18. Robert W. Malcolmson, "Dilemmas of the Nuclear Age," *Queen's Quarterly* 90 (Spring, 1983) esp. pp. 18-19.

19. See Thomas Weiskopf, "The Current Economic Crisis," *Socialist Review* 11 (May-June 1981), pp. 10-27.

20. James M. Cypher, "The Basic Economics of 'Rearming America'," *Monthly Review* 33 (November, 1981), pp. 11-27.

21. James M. Cypher, "Capitalist Planning and Military Expenditure," *Review of Radical Political Economics* 6 (Fall, 1974), pp. 1-19.

22. Michael T. Klare, *Beyond the Vietnam Syndrome: U.S. Intervention in the 1980s* (Washington, 1981); Paul Nitze, "Strategy in the Decade of

the 1980s," *Foreign Affairs* 59 (Fall, 1980), pp. 82-101; Richard Pipes, "Why the Soviet Union Thinks it can Fight and Win a Nuclear War," in Pipes, *U.S.-Soviet Relations in the Era of Detente* (New York, 1981), pp. 135-170 (originally written in 1977).

23. Joseph, "MAD to NUTS," esp. pp. 23-37; Rosenblum, "Who's Ahead: The U.S. or the USSR," in Regehr and Rosenblum, *Canada and the Nuclear Arms Race*, pp. 33-62; Arno J. Mayer, "The Cold War is Over," *Democracy* 2 (January, 1981), pp. 24-35.

24. On the quantities see Dan Smith, *The Defence of the Realm in the 1980s* (London, 1980); and Michael Pentz, *Towards the Final Abyss: The State of the Nuclear Arms Race* (Essex, 1980).

25. See Aldridge, "Deadly Race," in Wallis, *Waging Peace*, pp. 32-43.

26. For more detail on the first four developments see Joseph, "MAD to NUTS," pp. 23-56.

27. The March 1983 proposals were widely reported in the North American press. See "U.S. setting sights on futuristic defence," *Vancouver Sun*, 24 March 1983; and "Futuristic weapon plan called possible," *Globe and Mail*, 28 March 1983.

28. See Andrew Cockburn and Alexander Cockburn, "The Myth of Missile Accuracy," *New York Review of Books*, 20 November 1980; and Andrew Cockburn, "Cruise: the missile that does not work," *New Statesman*, 22 August 1980.

29. Charles Mann, "The Holocaust Lobby," *Mother Jones* (September-October, 1982) pp. 22-25, 47-50.

30. Thompson, *Beyond the Cold War*, p. 1.

31. Note the suggestive argument in Wayne Roberts, "Just as true to NATO," *Canadian Dimension* 15 (June-July, 1981), pp. 42-45; and the quote in "The Main Enemy is at Home," *Spartacist Canada* (May-June, 1982), p. 12.

32. *Globe and Mail*, 20 March 1982.

33. Marcy Darnovsky, "Let's Fake a Deal: A History of Arms Control," *Radical America* 16 (July-October, 1982), pp. 11; Robert Johansen, "The Failure of Arms Control; Why Government Efforts at Arms Control Have Failed," in Wallis, *Waging Peace*, pp. 71-79.

Nuclear Disarmament and Non-Alignment in Europe

Dan Smith

THE WESTERN EUROPEAN DISARMAMENT movements became a major political force in an upsurge of activism and concern in early 1980. Only in the Netherlands did a strong and well-established mass movement exist before that year. In other countries movements had flourished previously but were no longer vital political forces. In some countries, organizations existed before 1980, but not movements; in others, there was neither movement nor organization. For the most part, however, the disarmament movements have invented themselves, their organizational forms, their modes of struggle, and their policies in the midst of an intense period of work and campaigning. The result is an atmosphere of improvization, innovation, and not a little chaos.

One consequence of this is that it is often extremely difficult for outside observers to understand precisely what is happening inside the movements at any one time. Sometimes, of course, the problem is not a genuine difficulty in understanding but a deliberate misrepresentation of the movements' politics, aims, and strengths. But even for those who are sympathetically disposed, the disarmament movements often present a confusing picture. Perhaps the key to this problem is a common carelessness which leads people to talk about the Western European disarmament movement. There is no such thing, except in the vaguest sense—so vague that the term is no longer useful. Instead, there are many disarmament movements in Western Europe, and they differ from each other politically

and organizationally. In several countries, there is more than one movement and they may disagree on as many issues of strategy and orientation
as they agree upon. Diversity and variety are among the major characteristics of the disarmament movements in Western Europe.

When diversity and variety are ignored, one common misunderstanding promotes a small group of British disarmament activists into the
unwanted and unclaimed role of co-ordinators of all disarmament activism
in Western Europe. This group, European Nuclear Disarmament (END),
enjoys the limelight—especially in North America—for several reasons.
To begin with, one of its leaders, the English historian and writer E.P.
Thompson, is well known in North America. Possibly a more important
reason is that the Appeal for European Nuclear Disarmament, the founding statement of END issued in 1980, has been a key document of the disarmament movements, encapsulating many important ideas about the
significance of achieving even a small degree of nuclear disarmament in
Europe, and promoting a political perspective that is European without
being Eurocentric. A further reason is that END has organized and given
its name to a series of Conventions—Brussels in 1982, Berlin in 1983 and
Perugia, Italy, in 1984—which have been the major gathering points for
European and many non-European disarmament activists.

Whatever the reasons, misunderstanding should not be allowed to
flourish. END's role within the British disarmament movement and the
other movements in Western Europe has been a very particular one.

The Nature of the Movements

The European movements, as mass movements, base their strength on the
participation of large numbers of people in activities in local communities.
These activities are, for the most part, invisible to the national and international mass media, which tend to notice only very large demonstrations
and to believe, in the absence of big marches and rallies for a few months,
that the movements no longer exist. This merely reflects the failure or unwillingness of the media to understand the nature of mass movements and
of grassroots politics. As distinct from, for example, the freeze movement
in the United States, the Western European movements have usually been
better at generating their own leadership groups and staying away from a
focus on electoral and parliamentary politics, which tends to hand the
leadership positions to professional politicians. This is a source of
strength. Despite tensions between leaderships and sections of the
movements on many occasions, this tendency is also the source of a much

greater congruence between the leadership groups and the general membership of movements than one tends to find in organizations such as political parties and trade unions. It would be wrong to exaggerate or romanticize this: The movements do have leaders, stars, and even superstars; these groups and individuals do often develop different perspectives from those that predominate in the movements at large. But the problems are less and the leaderships more accountable than in most organizations and movements in recent political history.

Mass participation in the movements leads to a plethora of different styles and kinds of activity. It is the basis of the regenerative energy that the movements are capable of displaying. It is a necessary condition for the diversity within and among the movements, which is such an important characteristic of their politics. These connections—mass participation, energy, diversity—reflect the deep level of participation in the direction and activities of the movements. Local and regional branches of the movements organize autonomous actions of their own, set their own priorities, decide their own agendas, as well as acting upon priorities and agendas set by national leaderships. And the autonomy and diversity of practice are themselves linked to an autonomy of politics and philosophy of many different kinds.

Perhaps the outstanding example of this is the development of peace camps, especially women's peace camps, beginning with the one established in autumn 1981 at Greenham Common, one of the two UK bases for Cruise missiles. In Britain, the peace camps and their networks of supporters are not formally part of the Campaign for Nuclear Disarmament (CND), the major organization in British disarmament campaigning. They have established an independent and highly visible presence within the movement, which has also had the effect of directing attention towards the links between sexism and militarism—links that CND was unlikely to develop by itself. However, the peace camps are themselves but one feature in the multiplicity of different kinds of activity for disarmament in Britain. Campaigning for nuclear disarmament has not been restricted to any one form of political activity.

In their aims these diverse movements and currents within movements are unified in opposition to the deployment of the Cruise and Pershing II missiles in Western Europe. Deployment commenced in November 1983, but that has not closed the issue. Beyond that opposition (which the West German movement defined in its autumn 1983 campaign as the "minimal consensus"), the movements oppose the arms race and nuclear weapons in general. It should be noted that this wider opposition to nuclear weapons is not shared by all individuals and political groups who have opposed the introduction of Cruise and Pershing II missiles. For the movements, however, the resistance to the new missiles has generally been seen as merely the first item on an antinuclear agenda.

When we look at the details of the agenda, diversity reappears. It is not really possible to state the position of the Western European disarmament movements *in general* on a whole range of important issues. Some movements link opposition to nuclear weapons with opposition to nuclear power; others do not. Some extend antinuclear positions into a general anti-militarism; others do not. Some link opposition to NATO's nuclear weapons and strategy with opposition to NATO itself; others do not. Some demand a withdrawal from NATO; others concentrate on seeking the mutual dissolution of NATO and the Warsaw Pact; others do not appear to have confronted the issue of NATO involvement. Some link their concern about nuclear and military issues to a wider social critique; others do not.

The Major Trends: Unilateralism and Non-Alignment

In spite of the tremendous diversity of the Western European disarmament movements, there are certain major trends in all the countries where the movements are a major political force. Important among these trends is the developing feminist critique of militarism and power politics. Another important trend is the linkage between military confrontation in Europe and pressing issues of militarism and the use of armed force in the Third World. The trends I shall discuss here are those of unilateralism and non-alignment.

In their rejection of the rationales for deploying Cruise and Pershing II missiles, the disarmament movements have been unilateralist and unconditional. The call has not been for better negotiating positions at the Geneva arms control talks on Intermediate Nuclear Forces (INF); instead, the call has been for non-deployment on any terms. The basis for this has been fourfold.

First, arms control negotiations have a poor record of stopping or even marginally slowing the nuclear arms race. Second, when the Reagan administration got around to entering negotiations about INF, its negotiating positions were consistently and blatantly designed *not* to achieve an agreement with the USSR, but merely to contribute to the propaganda effort necessary to legitimate deployment of the missiles. Even if one believed arms control talks could, in principle, restrain, stop, or reverse the arms race, one could not believe that of the Geneva INF talks.

Third, the disarmament movements have necessarily developed a critique of nuclear weapons which is, among other things, moral and ethical. To condemn nuclear weapons as immoral but then to accept their continued possession (and continued threats and risks of their use) while diplomatic and secret talks drag on interminably is self-contradictory. Fourth, a unilateral action for disarmament is something a movement can demand of its own national government, in a political arena where it has some chance of exercising real influence. To develop mass support for disarmament actions, and then to place the locus of those actions outside of an accessible political arena is essentially to take the energy of the movements and throw it away.

In the European and Canadian context, this fourth basis for unilateralism has a particular meaning. This meaning is to be found in the idea of non-alignment, the perspective that alliance with either the United States or the USSR is, in principle, undesirable. In Western Europe as much as in North America, the term "unilateralism" is often used by opponents of the disarmament movements to discredit them. It has become, to some extent, a negative buzz-word. There has therefore been something of a search for an alternative word to express the same political intent. One word that has emerged to serve this purpose is "independent," encapsulating the idea that there could be Western European and Canadian actions for disarmament which do not depend on U.S. permission and which do not depend on being sanctioned by a U.S.-Soviet agreement.

The trends of unilateralism and non-alignment are therefore linked. Indeed, without a perspective of non-alignment, it is difficult to defend unilateralism against the charge that it is either inherently favourable to the USSR or means getting nuclear weapons out of your own country while still accepting the umbrella of a U.S. nuclear deterrent. However, the argument for non-alignment is a great deal more than a tactical debating point.

The Role of END

END has been one of the main carriers of non-alignment within the Western European disarmament movements. In the Appeal for European Nuclear Disarmament, the founders of END argued that there was a particular role for Europe in challenging the danger of nuclear war.[1] This role could be developed not simply through resisting the deployment of the Cruise and Pershing II missiles, but by rejecting the Cold War within Europe. It would be necessary for Europeans to become loyal not to East or West, but to each other. Communications across the East-West divide could be developed as a means of engendering a shared consciousness of the dangers and the possible paths out of danger.

One of the things that has made END particularly visible despite the fact that it has always been a relatively small group is that this perspective of a European disarmament strategy was popularized among groups and individuals throughout Europe. END was instrumental in linking an internationalist philosophy with an internationalist practice among the disarmament movements. Small visits, seminars, a variety of conferences, and the END conventions have been the main means of this development of internationalism.

END, however, has also made other distinctive contributions to the disarmament movements. First among these are the links that have been forged with the embattled independent peace and disarmament groups in Eastern Europe. These links have been made, despite great difficulties, to help strengthen those groups and to alert Western opinion to their existence. Second, END has probably been more forceful than most groups in the disarmament movements in criticizing Soviet nuclear strategy and military policies. This has not been done merely to demonstrate to the mass media that we are not Soviet pawns, nor is it a rejection of the disarmament movements' concentration on Western weapons and strategies. Rather, the intention has been to contribute to the development of a genuinely non-aligned philosophy, one which understands that U.S. culpability in the arms race does not exonerate Soviet actions. In the long term, END's most important contribution may turn out to be its effort to theorize and analyse non-alignment and the Cold War in Europe.

END is also associated with the view that one of the major factors legitimating and sustaining repression in Eastern Europe is military pressure from the West. Clampdowns on dissidents and independent peace groups in Eastern Europe in the wake of the initial deployment of Cruise and Pershing II missiles can be taken as confirmation of the accuracy of this view. Western politicians pose as friends of dissident opinion in Eastern Europe, lionizing Solidarnosc, for example, even though Reagan, Thatcher, and others would have found that movement's demands unacceptable in their own countries. At the same time, by launching a new Cold War against the USSR, those same politicians ensure that political space in Eastern Europe will continue to be severely restricted.

A political strategy of nuclear disarmament, of reducing confrontation between East and West, is the precondition for providing the possibility of some small increase in political space in Eastern Europe. The prospects there, even if this could be achieved, should not be overstated; reduced military confrontation is a necessary but far from a sufficient condition.

Non-alignment and U.S. Hegemony

The politics of non-alignment are therefore politics of greater democracy and reducing military confrontation. As such, they are also the politics of rejecting the military blocs in Europe. However, the blocs are far from being only instruments of confrontation; they are also instruments of political organization in both Eastern and Western Europe, ensuring Soviet dominance in its sphere and U.S. hegemony in its.

It is at this point in the argument that the connection between non-alignment and unilateralism, understood as including the meaning of independence, is clearest. Reducing military confrontation in Europe, and specifically achieving this through actions initiated on the Western side, would challenge the European positions of the superpowers. This challenge would be sharper in Western Europe because U.S. leadership is already under a profound and continuing challenge which predates the upsurge of the disarmament movements.

The issue here is the relative decline of the United States from the economic and political pre-eminence it achieved in the reordering of world power following the end of World War II. In part, this relative decline has resulted from developments in the Third World: the U.S. defeat in Vietnam, the success of other anti-imperialist struggles, and the growth in power of the oil exporting states in the 1970s. In part, the relative decline of the United States can be traced directly to the growth in Soviet military strength through the 1960s and 1970s and to its more activist world role. Finally, relative decline has also resulted from the success of economic and commercial competitors in Japan and Western Europe, with their faster rates of economic growth.

Tracing and bemoaning these problems in 1979, a special issue of the U.S. magazine *Business Week* set out an agenda for U.S. recovery.[2] A crucial item was a major military buildup, based on increases in U.S. military spending but including the allies/competitors in a newly intensified effort against the USSR. The rationale was straightforward: The economic lead of the United States had declined; its political leadership was no longer accepted unquestioningly; but its strategic predominance *over its allies* remained. By stressing how dependent Japan and Western Europe were on the United States for strategic security, the United States could impose a new political discipline among the advanced capitalist states, from which it could then benefit economically. The *Business Week* agenda has defined U.S. policy from the latter part of the Carter administration until now.

Despite the risks and costs, therefore, it does not seem that the United States can at present be thought of as having any real interest in a

reduction of military confrontation with the USSR. Rather, the precise op-
posite is true. The new Cold War conforms to current U.S. interests. If the
costs and risks come to appear to be too great, as well they ought to, the
alternative for the United States is the graceful acceptance of declining
power.

While Western European governments have, by and large, accepted
the new Cold War they have not yet bought the accompanying logic of
U.S. economic hegemony. That may come, but for the moment rivalry and
antagonisms between the United States and the Western European states
remain essentially unaffected. Indeed, Ronald Reagan cannot even count
on Margaret Thatcher in disputes over economic policies. The basic
political and economic trajectory in Western Europe has been away from
the dependence on and subordination to the United States which
characterized the post-1945 reconstruction.

We are, then, at a period of crisis in the genuine sense of the word: at
least potentially, a turning point. It is also a period of crisis in the Chinese
sense of the word. As others have pointed out, the Chinese character for
"crisis" combines "danger" and "opportunity". The dangers are evident:
resurgent U.S. militarism, interventionism in the Third World, a spiralling
nuclear arms race, response in kind from a brutal and insecure USSR, and
at worst a nuclear war. But the opportunity also exists. The Western European disarmament movements have become major political forces in part
because they sit in the mainstream of Western European politics in spite of
their radical styles and policies. To the erosion of U.S. economic
dominance and political leadership, they have added rejection of U.S.
strategic leadership. Whether or not it is an explicit part of their politics
and slogans, the disarmament movements implicitly stand as an opposition
force against the reassertion of U.S. leadership. The mass of NATO's
nuclear weapons are U.S. owned. NATO nuclear strategy is defined by
U.S. capabilities and strategic concepts. In Western Europe, to oppose
nuclear weapons, and especially to do so unilaterally, is to oppose the existence and the strengthening of the U.S.-led military bloc. From that position, non-alignment flows naturally.

The Development of Long-Term Perspectives

This analysis goes some way towards explaining why, despite the obvious
dangers, it is so hard to make progress against nuclear confrontation. At
one level, the issues raised by movements for nuclear disarmament are
human and universal—they concern survival, basic issues of morality, and
equally basic issues about the utilization of resources. One might expect it

to be simply a matter of time, and of not too much time, before the cogency of arguments for disarmament are fully assimilated and acted upon.

But those are not the only issues raised. Crucially, nuclear weapons are components in networks of power and domination. Thus, pressingly urgent though the issue of nuclear disarmament is, it is also one in which progress can never be quick or easy and in which all thoughts of change must be directed towards long-term perspectives.

Non-alignment is itself a long-term perspective. It also has to be admitted that it is one which is rather vague, in which the content is only slowly becoming clear as we try to think our way beyond the blocs, beyond nuclear confrontation. As a long-term perspective, non-alignment does not, so far at least, automatically lead to any particular policy proposal. For example, within the non-aligned groups and movements debates continue about how to address the issue of membership in NATO: Some argue for unconditional withdrawal from the alliance, others seek a process of change from within. Or again, in terms of defence policy there is a great variety of proposals for non-nuclear, non-provocative measures, including both military and non-violent means. How non-aligned Western European states would relate to the Third World or, indeed, to the United States and the Soviet Union is an issue which maps out a further terrain for continuing debate.

In broad terms, it is clear that non-alignment and unilateral/independent disarmament policies are closely connected. It is clear also that what is sought is a changed and more independent relationship with the United States and a less confrontational relationship with the USSR. But these are the broad terms; the details remain to be identified and debated. A perspective of non-alignment, then, though a necessary part of the politics of disarmament movements, does not come into the world holding all the answers to the questions which may be asked of it. As the disarmament movements of Western Europe continue to develop, so they will continue to invent their politics.

Notes

1. The END Appeal can be found, among other places, in E.P. Thompson and Dan Smith, eds., *Protest and Survive* (Harmondsworth, 1980; New York, 1981).

2. "The decline of US power," *Business Week*, 12 March 1979.

Towards a True North-South Dialogue

Pierre Beaudet

IN NORTH AMERICA and particularly in Europe the peace movements are a major expression of the attempt of social activists to change the economic and political status quo. In the countries generally known as the Third World, the main force seeking to transform society has been the national liberation movements.[1] There are many differences between the peace and national liberation movements, and there are extreme differences in the societies that have given them birth. But the growing internationalization of political and economic structures and common, if underlying, features of both, suggest that each has much to contribute to the other. Over time there is a need for convergence.

In North America and Europe, the peace movements are primarily oriented towards the East-West conflict and the growing threat of nuclear holocaust. Although this conflict also exists in the Third World, there the main issue is the North-South polarization: Oppressed and exploited societies are rebelling against the imperialist powers. This difference in focus constitutes the first obstacle to convergence.

On a more political level, the national liberation struggles captured the attention of the protest movements of the sixties and seventies in the advanced capitalist countries. Radical nationalism in the South nurtured a whole generation of youth hungry for new revolutionary models. Since the eighties, however, a new political generation in the North has been expressing itself through various social movements, including the peace movement. This generation has new terms of reference and new political sensibilities which, though not excluding dialogue with the liberation movements, are not preoccupied with struggles against imperialism.

This distancing is also the result of a certain disillusionment with the evolution of post-revolutionary societies in the Third World. As René Dumont explains in *Finis les lendemains qui chantent*,[2] the image of the heroic Third World cannot compete against the political and ideological counteroffensive of imperialism in the era of Rambo and Reagan, particularly given the demobilization of the activists of the sixties and seventies.

Nonetheless, anyone in the North struggling for peace is well aware that the question of war and peace is now being played out in El Salvador, in Lebanon, and in South Africa. And so in the United States, the imperialist power *par excellence*, there are strong links between peace activists and supporters of the struggle in Central America. In Europe and Canada a similar tendency can be seen.

There are three basic reasons why the convergence of the peace movement and the national liberation movements is desirable. First there are moral reasons. The struggle against oppression in the South is connected to the struggle for peace in the North because both confront issues of violence. The peace movement is concerned with the direct violence of war. The struggle in the South is against both direct violence and the violence of economic exploitation. As a statement from an international conference of non-governmental organizations puts it, "There can be no peace if only direct violence is abolished, because economic exploitation will recreate the violence."[3]

Then there are economic reasons. Dozens of studies have detailed how the cycle of militarization in the North is closely linked to the defence of "empires" in the South, often through terrorist dictatorships which impose themselves through violence.[4] The pillaging of the Third World is tied in with the war economies of the North. All efforts for peace will be in vain if the structural links in the imperialist chains are not broken.

Finally, there are political reasons. Caught between the United States and the USSR, peace organizations are trying to establish new alliances. Perhaps their most promising allies are the oppressed peoples and their liberation movements. This alliance is essential to develop the strength to stand up to the great powers.

The convergence of the peace movement and the liberation movements will be the outcome of a dialogue that fosters a mutual understanding of areas of both commonality and difference.

The Potential Contribution of the Liberation Movements

In most Third World countries, state systems and structures are imposed through direct violence. For example, in the Central American countries of El Salvador, Guatemala, or Honduras the legal political structures are little more than window-dressing for terrorist machines representing the tiny minority of ruling families. Empires practice what Jean Ziegler calls "the negation of the peoples as possible subject of a national history".[5] When the dominant classes do not exclude large numbers of people from society through outright racism, as in South Africa, they rationalize their exclusion by a kind of "social racism". The effects of this situation take various forms: genocide against the Indians of Guatemala, massive extermination of dissidents in Argentina and Turkey, expropriation of territory and mass expulsions in South Africa and Palestine, or the near enslavement of labour by the denial of all rights.

The frightful misery which results, as Réne Dumont explains, goes unchecked in a civil society reduced to its simplest expression, that of a militarized society divided into two entrenched camps.[6] In order to resist extermination, grassroots movements then begin a process of self-defence. This process leads to the birth of liberation movements.

Popular self-defence becomes the only possible response to the super-militarized terrorist states. However, this process of organization takes various forms, in some cases legal, in others militarized. In recent years, many liberation movements have concluded that they have militarized the popular struggle too quickly, substituting themselves de facto for a deeper and more massive mobilization. A certain "fixation with the idea of armed struggle as the only revolutionary form" has led to many problems, such as in the Palestinian case.[7] Today, however, the fronts which come together in the liberation movements often take the form of mass movements for self-organization and self-defence. This is seen most clearly in South Africa and El Salvador.

Faced with violent extermination by the enemy, the liberation movements are adopting original forms of struggle. In South Africa the African National Congress is both the prime mover of mass protests such as strikes and the organizer of the armed struggle. The ANC was founded in 1912 on the philosophy of Gandhi, who carried out his first campaigns in South Africa, and who said, "When the only choice is between cowardice and violence, we must opt for the violent solution.[8] In this case, as in El Salvador, the mass fronts have not substituted themselves for grassroots organization (as occurred in many guerrilla movements of the sixties and seventies) but have merged with the liberation movement.

In Third World countries directly occupied by foreign armies, guerrilla warfare—"the war of the masses of an economically backward country rising up against an army of occupation"[9]—is the universally recognized form of passage from political struggle to violent struggle. As one theorist of insurrection, Leon Trotsky, explains, this process depends "one-tenth on purely military leadership and nine-tenths on political preparation."[10] The liberation movements in China, Vietnam, Guinea-Bissau, and Algeria were successful because "they based their strategy on the patient construction of a political infrastructure based in the population".[11]

The liberation movements' process of reflection on the forms and rhythms of struggle can therefore teach the peace movement certain strategic and tactical principles. In order to make gains, the peace movement must learn "the art of strategy", drawing inspiration from people's war, which "should, like a kind of vapoury essence, never condense into a solid body".[12]

Nationalism and Internationalism

The struggle of the peace movement, like that of the liberation movements, is internationalist in character. In practice, however, liberation movements are also national movements cutting across class boundaries. This national dimension is fundamental since it allows the achievement of a broad union of all the forces opposed to domination and exploitation. At the same time, however, the interests of a particular group may diverge from the general interest. In fact, once they have come to power, liberation movements are often confronted with the reason of state, which by giving "priority to the preservation of gains, runs counter to the feeling that there should be absolute solidarity among all subjugated nations and people, and breaks the movement."[13]

The desire for universal freedom coexists with a field of real social forces, and this fact must be recognized, not mystified. If a national consensus is not achieved by the movement, it cannot build the strength necessary to resist the terrorist state. Afterwards, the national consensus becomes a trap, and alliances, compromises and negotiations become necessary. China abandons Vietnam and Vietnam abandons Kampuchea. Mozambique negotiates with South Africa at the expense of the ANC. Tomorrow, will Nicaragua be able to resist American pressure to abandon the FMLN (Farabundo Marti Liberation Front) of El Salvador?

This contradiction inherent in political activity can be resolved, and here the experience of the liberation movements can enlighten us. The first lesson is the necessity of counting on one's own forces, the second involves putting aside a certain revolutionary romanticism. The revolution may be "permanent", but it goes through stages; it experiences lulls. Those liberation movements which have been successful were able to identify how far grassroots mobilization could be sustained and those who were not able to do so were defeated. Populations always fight for historically-determined objectives, according to their level of politicization and organization. These objectives cannot be successfully imposed from above.

Pluralism and Democracy

In the context of societies dominated by imperialist powers through terrorist states, liberation movements serve as social laboratories for experiments in people's democracy. Liberation movements always represent broad social coalitions and the diversity of interests implies a pluralism of ideas. However, the process of militarization restricts this experimentation by the de facto denial of real freedom ("freedom is always the freedom of the one who thinks differently," said Rosa Luxembourg[14]). And once power has been achieved, the logic of state power also tends towards centralization and a reduction of diversity.

However, in some cases liberation movements have been able to resist, however precariously, the stifling of democracy. In Central America, movements such as the FMLN in El Salvador have succeeded in bringing together large numbers of grassroots organizations and political parties without setting up a centralized leadership, and they have done this while recognizing the need to co-ordinate military actions. The FSLN (Sandinista National Liberation Front) in Nicaragua, while not the perfect model, is experimenting in its own way with original forms of mass mobilization.[15] Similarly, the attachment of the Palestinian movement to the integrity and autonomy of the Palestinian Liberation Organization is an obstacle to the efforts of authoritarian states in the region (such as Syria and Libya) to stifle its highly democratic nature.[16]

Many liberation movements have resisted the temptation to be transformed into classical Marxist-Leninist parties, "which obscure and deny the symbolic identities and specific cultural wealth of ancestral peoples".[17] The appeal to specific traditions (Sandinism in Nicaragua, Amilcar Cabral in Africa) is a defence, though sometimes an ambiguous one, against rigid models and dogmatism, and thus an encouragement to democracy and freedom.

The Religious Aspect

In many liberation movements, the religious aspect is often very important. In El Salvador, Christian base communities take part in the war of liberation within the ranks of the grassroots and revolutionary organizations. They consider this participation as

> part of Christian life and as a response to God, who, at the present time, asks them to put into practice His message of salvation. Their opting for people's war is based on the impossibility of obtaining peace through dialogue, which is blocked by an illegitimate government in violation of the common good.[18]

The religious factor is also an expression of the freedom and pluralism of the liberation movements. Christianity, like Shi'ite and Sunni Islam, belongs to the symbolic universe, to the imagination of an ideal of justice and brotherly love, and is a form of opposition to all powers. For religion has a precise social function, as Marx said, "the expression of real distress and also the protest against real distress".[19] It brings into the liberation movements an ethical critique that constitutes a bulwark against the formation of new oppressive elites. The experience of the Christian base communities in Latin America and elsewhere has certainly been an encouragement to the development of a critical "people's church" in the countries of the North. The peace movement has taken advantage of this by allying itself with the Christian protest against war.

The Potential Contribution of the Peace Movements

The peace movement that has been developing since the late 1970s is a dynamic laboratory of social change. Trying to avoid premature and exaggerated generalizations, we can identify a number of features on which convergence with the liberation movements can be contemplated.

The peace movement represents a variety of experiences. This diversity is most evident in Europe, particularly in the Federal Republic of Germany (FRG) where the movement has grown vigorously. It can be said that the movement in Europe has three major components. First, there are the groups affiliated with the parties of the left, the social democratic parties, the communist parties, and the trade unions. This is the most traditional component in the sense that it constitutes a pressure group for the parties of the left, for the peace plank of their programs. This model is close to that of British groups such as the CND, the Campaign for Nuclear Disarmament.

The second component is the Christian wing. In the FRG, the demands of groups such as Christians for Disarmament and Pax Christi are humanistic, pacifist, and radical.[20] In Holland, the Christian wing, the Interchurch Council for Peace, is the moving force in a peace movement that is very strong.[21]

The third component of the peace movement consists of the so-called alternatives, with the Green Party at the centre. This component especially has been the source of important political discussion. I am going to concentrate on this heterogeneous wing.

Militarism and Capitalism

The dynamic of the peace movement connected with the Greens in the FRG is that of a global, radical protest movement:

> A radical reorganization of our short-sighted economic rationality is essential. We do not accept that the present economy of waste promotes happiness and a fulfilling life. On the contrary, people are becoming more and more agitated and unfree. Only if we free ourselves from overvaluing the material standard of living, if we can make possible self-fulfillment and bear in mind the boundaries of our nature, will our creative forces also be freed for reshaping life on an ecological basis.[22]

According to this option, the militarism of today's society is not an aberration, but evidence of the crisis of a society whose basic conflicts lead to the most destructive confrontations. On a strictly economic level, more than 20 per cent of the productive capacity of the United States, for example, is given to arms production.[23] The struggle for peace, therefore, implies a radically different social and economic rationality, as Rudolf Bahro explains:

> Not only does the requirement for general and complete military disarmament remain indispensible, but it must be backed up by a program of industrial disarmament, i.e., in constructive terms, a program of industrial conversion [as the] basis for continuing efforts to convert the ways of thinking of the majority of the population.[24]

To put an end to the present state of affairs, the peace movement connected with the Greens calls for a struggle which goes beyond "the short-term interests of the workers", since, according to Bahro:

> Socialism today is much more than a workers' and union movement of the traditional kind. The struggle for an equitable redistribution of the social product between the wage earners and the bosses of the rich "Western" in-

dustrialized states always takes place at the expense of the rest of humanity. We cannot go on acting as if the general future depended upon the outcome of the class struggles going on within each country for real wages and for which party is better to be entrusted with control of the State. The contrasts which follow the North/South and East/West axes are inextricably linked, and encroach significantly on those problems.[25]

So we can see that for the Greens, the struggle for peace is part of the global struggle against the status quo. It cannot, and should not, become the tool of political parties or factions which try to make the peace issue just another issue. This development parallels the attempts of many liberation movements to escape the internal forces which tend to limit the goals of these movements for social transformation by trying to co-opt the gains of the struggle.

Other Organizational Models, Other Political Models

The Greens have emerged out of a long political process. Growing out of the German extra-parliamentary movement of the seventies, the Greens are attempting:

> to constitute a learning ground for direct democracy, starting from concrete interests (and no longer from abstract principles), working their way back, step by step, to the basic causes of the evils and deficiencies resulting from the way society is organized; they propose a gradual restructuring, starting at the periphery, not only of political activism, but also of grassroots organization, towards the ultimate goal of generalized self-management, both in life and in work.[26]

The approach of the Greens is an important step towards the reappropriation of political space. In Germany, as in the other Western countries, the left of the 1970s had reached a sort of theoretical dead-end, following the waning of activism and the stalemate in the debate over reformism (identified with parliamentary action) versus revolution (mass action). The Greens are attempting to develop a new concept of the movement, of the party as:

> collective understanding rather than an apparatus of the State...a vehicle for the body politic as a whole, for its understanding of the problems of social evolution, [which should] offer an example of the human progress for which it is working.[27]

They seek to offer a concrete utopia which, in a sense, fulfills the classic definition of political action formulated by Marx: ''The working class has no ideals to realize, but to set free the elements of the new society with which old collapsing bourgeois society itself is pregnant."[28]

On a more organizational level, this new movement is attempting to reinforce horizontal structures, networks of initiative and action, rather than policies formulated solely at the top:

> We have decided to form a new type of party organization, the basic struc-
> tures of which are set up in a grassroots-democratic and decentralized
> way.... [This is expressed through] the continuous control of all office
> holders, delegates and institutions by the rank and file...together with
> replaceability at any time so as to make organization and policy transparent
> to everyone and to counter the dissociation of individuals from their base.[29]

These efforts also go towards enlarging the social base of the Greens, which is still very concentrated among petit bourgeois intellectuals and marginal elements. To bring together these elements with other groups in society—in particular the working class—the movement must propose original forms of political action.

Rethinking structures leads also to rethinking means, and to the attempt to define the relation between mass extra-parliamentary action and the occupation of institutional political space. (There are now 28 Green members in the Bundestag and dozens of Greens elected provincially and municipally.) Many among the Greens are rather sceptical about the possibilities for action in the institutional political sphere, but the general opinion is that "uncompromising anti-electoralism is, in a way, a sort of electoralist fixation. These people, unconsciously, expect too much from this kind of work, just as some expect too much from mass struggle."[30]

The Technocratic Myth

Many peace organizations have strived to achieve a meeting of socialism, pacifism, feminism, and the ecology movement. New enquiries have been made into the modes of social production, resulting in the questioning of the models of development applied in Western countries and imposed on the Third World. The Greens are asking if it is possible to stop "the pillage of nature [which] brings about long-term damage".[31] They are calling for a struggle against purely quantitative growth and in favour of a qualitative growth to be achieved "with equal or reduced use of energy and processing of raw materials".[32]

In the Third World, the shortage of the most basic goods and services leads to a fascination with the Western model of consumer society. Liberation movements are confronted with this problem after victory, when some sectors of the population expect rapid changes based on the Western model. Because the resources do not exist, and also because this model leads to the reproduction of social, economic, and political inequalities, many liberation movements are deeply concerned with development models. The point is to construct a model for the transformation of social production and not just to distribute the existing social production better. Thus in Nicaragua the FSLN is trying to reorient agriculture towards the production of food resources more adapted to local needs using methods that require fewer chemical and mechanical inputs. In Great Britain, at the Lucas Aerospace plant, the fight for the conversion of production away from armaments has led to a rethinking of the hierarchy of positions and salaries and the division of labour as a whole.

Against the State Control of Society—For the Social Control of the State

Certain peace organizations are used by political parties in their fight for power. (This is the case in France, for example, except for a minority movement, the Comité pour le désarmement nucléaire en Europe.) In the FRG, the Greens are trying to avoid this path; hence the persistent criticism and mistrust of electoralism. The Greens do this with caution: In many cases the struggle against the state, instead of leading to the gradual suppression of the state in favour of free associations, has given way to the suppression of constitutional rights and liberties. The Greens are trying to strike a balance between the state and the constitutional rights connected with it, and to develop the greatest possible space for civil society. At this time, according to Rudolf Bahro, the role of the movement should be:

> to offer the support of transcendent practice and revolutionary behaviour. This [movement], a constructive counter-power but a revolutionary one, must influence the system of forces and the social organization, and remind the state hierarchy of its limits. Basically, this means a division of social power, and setting up a dialectic between the state and social forces.... The result is a situation of dual power and the progressive reduction of the power of the state.[33]

Not only the Greens have had this concern. For example, in 1980, FRELIMO, the liberation movement in power in Mozambique, decided to accentuate the separation between the structures of the party and those of the state in order to re-invigorate civil society and encourage it to exert pressure on state structures.

Other International Alliances

The Greens and the other main elements of the peace movement in Europe pursue a foreign policy of determined non-alignment. Their goal is to establish an independent, demilitarized (which does not mean without defence), nuclear-free Europe. This Europe would be allied with forces in the Third World which share the same goals.

This implies a firm critique of the USSR, not only for its imperialist practices throughout the world (Eritrea, Afghanistan, Poland), but also for the kind of societal model promoted by the Soviet Communist Party. The Greens also put a lot of emphasis on links with the independent peace movements and other movements in Eastern Europe. This position is completely opposed to the pro-Western rhetoric about the USSR and the supposed danger of massive aggression on its part. Again in the words of Rudolf Bahro:

> The Russians will not take the offensive since, historically, it has been the Soviet empire which has had its back to the wall; it has completely failed in its goal, dating back to the October Revolution, to catch up with and surpass capitalism. The root of the problem is profit, and even if it exists in the East, it is on this side, the West, where the motor is turning. And it is on this side that the spiral of the arms race must be broken, even if we are not sure the Soviets will disarm immediately.[34]

At the same time, the Third World liberation movements are attempting to diversify their international alliances, even though the weapons of struggle against terrorist regimes most often come to them from the USSR.[35] In 1981 in West Germany, the peace organizations took part in a campaign to collect funds to buy arms for the guerrillas in El Salvador. This gesture, though symbolic, points up the importance of action rather than moral support or strictly humanitarian aid. The program of the Greens also expresses support for "popular resistance against regimes which practise open or structural violence".[36]

Towards A New International Alliance

Against the power of the status quo the peace and liberation movements are trying to demonstrate that changes in the balance of power are possible. After all, the oppressive empires are now in decline, both in Central America and Africa. Moreover, in the Western countries, as in the East, society is becoming more and more critical of the state and the established political structures.

If this does not take the form of mass protest movements it is largely because the movements which historically have been the vehicle for protest—the traditional left made up of the socialist, social democratic, and communist parties—no longer seem to meet the expectations of the people. The general disarray of the left stems from the absence of an alternative political and social program, an absence which is just beginning to be filled by the various alternative movements, peace movements, and liberation movements.

Today, the legitimacy of the power of many states is on the decline. The continuous invasions of the streets by the Brazilians and Argentinians, the food riots that rock the Maghreb countries, the expansion of the people's insurrections in El Salvador, Namibia, the Philippines, Afghanistan, and elsewhere are evidence of the discrediting of the imperialist powers. The disenchantment is just as great in the United States, Great Britain, France, or Quebec. This is not the coming of a great social upheaval, or a revolutionary situation per se, but more a profound split between society and the state which can as easily come out in rage as in passivity and indifference.

What becomes ever clearer is the absurdity of a system with the productive capacity to solve all the basic material problems of the world but which uses this capacity to build arms and prepare for war. One hour of arms spending is equivalent to the total cost of a world campaign to totally eliminate the major epidemics of the world. Meanwhile millions of people are unemployed while a large part of the world's productive capacity is unused and most of humanity lacks the most basic of goods.

The meeting of the peace movement and the liberation movements is one way out of this stalemate. They are united by the first demand of any social protest movement: the right to democracy and to life. Both movements tend to go beyond the overly restrictive framework of individual rights to demand the "right to struggle to overcome injustice, the right to self-defence, to the defence of one's being, not of one's property, but one's own violated being".[37]

The peace movement, like the liberation movements, is trying to draw on two contradictory principles. On the one hand is the Promethean ethic of intransigent struggle against injustice, to guard against attempts to co-opt and corrupt. On the other hand is the need for an alternative *realpolitik* which can win, that is, which can enlarge the areas of freedom and democracy available to people. As Agnes Heller points out:

> Radical leftists are not ones to be content with the role of scout, though they are that too; they are those who recognize the reality of all human

needs, with the exception of those which involve the oppression and exploitation of others.... Radical leftists know that the only real social objective is one that is recognized as such by the majority of people, one to which the majority would be prepared to make as much of a commitment as they do to the satisfaction of their own needs.[38]

Notes

1. The expression "Third World" has an ideological dimension that distorts reality. There is really nothing in common among, for example, Brazil, Mali, and South Africa except that they are societies controlled to one degree or another from the outside.

2. René Dumont, *Finis les lendemains qui chantent* (Paris, 1983).

3. Chris Pinney, *International Conference of NGO's on disarmament and development*, ICDA, Brussels, April 1982.

4. See, among others, various documents from the Catholic Organization for Development and Peace.

5. Jean Ziegler, *Contre l'ordre du monde, les rebelles* (Paris, 1983), p. 145.

6. René Dumont, *Finis les lendemains*. See also, by the same author, *Le mal développement en Amérique latine* (Paris, 1982), and *L'Afrique étranglée* (Paris, 1981).

7. Eqbal Ahmad, "The PLO Split," *Merip Reports*, December 1983.

8. Gandhi, *Tous les hommes sont frères* (Paris, 1969).

9. V.N. Giap, *Guerre du peuple, armée du peuple* (Paris, 1967), p. 44.

10. Leon Trotsky, "Où va la France?", *Quatrième internationale*, 1958.

11. Gérard Chaliand, *Mythes révolutionnaires du Tiers-Monde* (Paris, 1976), p. 103.

12. Carl von Clausewitz, *On War*, trans. Col. J.J. Graham (London, 1962), vol. 2, p. 346.

13. Jean Ziegler, *Main basse sur l'Afrique* (Paris, 1976), p. 274.

14. Quoted in Paul Frolich, *Rosa Luxembourg* (Paris, 1965).

15. Claudio Thomas Bornstein, "Quelques idées sur la révolution nicaraguéene," *Cahiers du Cedal*, no. 5, 1983.

16. Pierre Beaudet, "L'"après Beyrouth' en Cisjordonie et à Gaza," *Cahiers du CEAD*, April 1984.

18. Hugo Cancino Troncoso, *Christianisme et révolution*, Dossier de l'ALAI, 1982.

19. Karl Marx, *Contribution to the Critique of Hegel's Philosophy of Law*, Introduction, in Karl Marx and Friedrich Engels, *Collected Works* (New York, 1975), vol. 3, p. 175.

20. *Der Spiegel*, 15 June, 1981.

21. Jeanne Brunschwig, "Les Mouvements pour la paix," *Cahiers du Forum pour l'indépendance et la paix*, été 1983.

22. *Programme of the Green Party*, preface by Jonathan Porritt (London, 1983), p. 6.

23. Ernest Mandel, "The Threat of War and the Struggle for Socialism," *New Left Review*, no. 141, September 1983.

24. R. Bahro, "Réflexions pour un nouveau départ du mouvement pacifiste en Allemagne," *Tribune Socialiste*, commission internationale du PSU, May 1982.

25. "Speech by R. Bahro at the Federal Convention of the 'Greens' ", Offenbach, November 1979, published in *A l'est, du nouveau* (Syros, 1980).

26. Philippe Ivernel, "Le Parti Vert, quatrième parti établi ou facteur de déstabilisation?" *Tribune Internationale*.

27. R. Bahro, *L'Alternative* (Paris, 1979).

28. Karl Marx, *The Civil War in France*, in Karl Marx and Friedrich Engels, *Selected Works* (Moscow, 1968), p. 295.

29. *Programme*, pp. 8-9.

30. *Alternatives* Magazine, no. 1, 1983; quote is from an interview with Rainer Esche, elected member from the "Alternative List" in West Berlin, the Berlin counterpart of the Greens.

31. *Programme*, p. 9.

32. *Programme*, p. 10.

33. R. Bahro, *L'Alternative*.

34. R. Bahro, *Cahiers du Forum pour l'indépendance et la paix*.

35. Jean Ziegler, *Contre l'ordre.*

36. *Programme*, p. 29.

37. Ignacio Ellacuria, ''Droits de l'homme, évolution et utopie,'' *Amérique latine*, no. 2, April.

38. Agnès Heller, *Marxisme et démocratie* (Paris, 1981), p. 227.

The Soviet Union and the Peace Movement

David Mandel

THE NATURE AND DEGREE of Soviet responsibility for the arms race is one of the most disputed and complex questions before the peace movement. NATO's ultimate justification for its arms escalation has always been the "Soviet threat" to the West. In its turn, the peace movement is accused of dangerous naivité and of being the dupe, if not the agent, of Moscow.

Even though the movement condemns both Soviet and U.S. aims and even though it maintains ties with the independent peace groups in the East, the major currents of the peace movement in Western Europe and, to a lesser degree, in North America, demand disarmament by NATO independent of reciprocal actions by the Warsaw Pact. In practice, they demand unilateral actions from their own governments to reduce and end their participation in the arms race; at the same time they reject the accusation of "working for Moscow" and insist that theirs is a non-aligned position.

Whether this combination of unilateralism and non-alignment is a valid strategy or merely a smoke screen depends ultimately on the analysis one makes of Soviet foreign policy and its role in the arms race. For it seems evident that if one accepts the official Western version of the Soviet threat, the accusations directed against the peace movement have a certain logic. It becomes more and more important then, to analyse the foreign policy of the Soviet Union and its role in the arms race, and to use that analysis to evaluate the stance of the Western antiwar and disarmament movements towards the USSR.

NATO Arguments and the Realities of Soviet Foreign Policy

NATO's strategy is directed against, and justified by, the "Soviet threat". We are told that there exists on the part of the USSR, if not the imminent danger of an invasion of the West, then at least the threat of blackmail, which, in the end, comes down to the same thing. When the Canadian army goes out on manoeuvres, the Red Army is the imaginary enemy.

The idea that the Soviet Union has aggressive designs against the West is a premise that is only rarely questioned by our information media. Journalists focus almost exclusively on the military-technical aspects of East-West relations: Is it really true that the Russians are stronger? What kinds of weapons do they have, and where and how are they deployed? The realities of Soviet foreign policy are completely neglected. Instead, the spectre of the world revolution is evoked. This, at least, has the merit of being a political argument of sorts. And so at the first press conference after his inauguration President Reagan declared:

> I know of no leader of the Soviet Union, since the Revolution and in-
> cluding the present leadership, that has not more than once repeated in the
> various Communist congresses they hold, their determination that their
> goal must be the promotion of world revolution and a one-world Socialist
> or Communist state.... They reserve the right to commit any crime, to lie,
> to cheat, in order to obtain it.[1]

Yet if one chooses to examine the Soviet historical record since the second half of the 1920s, it turns out that the Soviet Union has, in fact, made an invaluable contribution to the prevention of revolution, above all in the developed capitalist countries, where it accords an absolute priority to the maintenance and development of diplomatic, trade, and other relations.[2]

In reality, even the most casual study of the Soviet government indicates that revolution in the West is the last thing it desires. Indeed, the central goal of Soviet foreign policy since the war has been to get the West to accept the status quo in Europe.[3] Not only would revolution upset this status quo with unpredictable consequences but, if China is any indication, any revolution that offers the Soviet people a socialist model that is possibly more attractive than the existing Soviet system constitutes a moral danger to the ruling bureaucracy. It is this threat that explains the implacable hostility of the Soviet regime to Solidarnosc and, 12 years earlier, to the Prague Spring.

But what about the "Sovietization" of Eastern Europe? Soviet domination of these countries clearly merits condemnation by all who sincerely value freedom. Nevertheless, it has little to do with alleged aspirations to dominate the West or to spread revolution throughout the world. At Yalta, at the end of World War II, Churchill and Roosevelt recognized the Soviet Union's right to have friendly states as its Western neighbours. These states were to act as a barrier against Germany, a country that had invaded the Soviet Union twice in less than a quarter of a century, inflicting tremendous human and material losses. Once this right was conceded, it was, or should have been, obvious that the only way for the Stalinist regime to assure the diplomatic loyalty of the East European states, especially in the face of the rising Cold War and the Western pressure aimed at breaking them away from the Soviet Union, was to install regimes in its own image and under its tutelage.

To explain is by no means to justify. But one must be wary of the use of Eastern Europe as evidence of Soviet designs on the West. Soviet control of Eastern Europe plays an essentially military and defensive role vis-à-vis the West. The economic benefits that the Soviet Union obtains from it are negligible compared to the subsidy that it has been paying, especially during the past 15 to 20 years—$18.6 billion U.S. in 1981 alone, according to the estimate of a Western economist.[4] It is also a costly empire on the political level, causing inestimable damage to the Soviet Union's international image and exposing its own people to the anti-bureaucratic virus that rages from time to time in that part of the world. (It is easier for citizens of Eastern Europe to travel to the West than to the Soviet Union, where they are viewed with suspicion as potential carriers of this disease.)

In light of this experience with Eastern Europe, the idea that the Soviet Union would like to, or could, take over the West, seems laughable. Moreover, the spokespersons of NATO never mention that the USSR withdrew its forces from Finland at the end of the war and later from Austria in exchange for the neutrality of these states. Yet Finland, except that it cannot join military alliances, probably enjoys more independence vis-à-vis the Soviet Union than Canada does vis-à-vis its own neighbour to the south. Stalin tried several times to negotiate the reunification of Germany—on a capitalist basis—also in return for its neutrality. The United States, however, was not prepared to give up, in central Europe, so potentially powerful an ally against the Soviet Union as West Germany.[5]

In contrast, Afghanistan does constitute, in part at least, a new stage in Soviet foreign policy. For the first time, the Soviet Army was sent into a country that is not part of the Soviet barrier to its west. But just like the states of Eastern Europe, Afghanistan shares a border (over 1,000 kilometres) with the Soviet Union as well as with other states that are hostile to the Soviet Union (particularly China and Pakistan). At the time of the invasion, Afghanistan had already been ruled for three years by a pro-Soviet Communist regime that was recognized by the West. Whatever finally impelled the Soviets to intervene, it is now generally agreed that this was not part of a master strategy aimed at the oil reserves of the Middle East.[6]

Soviet policy towards Third World countries has generally been bolder than towards the developed capitalist states. The Soviet Union since Stalin has sought to increase its influence in the Third World but has always acted with enough caution to avoid direct confrontation with the United States. Its conduct, which seeks allies and clients, is not so different from that of the United States, except that it does not go as far as the United States—it has no systemic reason for doing so. The United States claims for itself the right to world leadership; its definition of prosperity requires free access to markets worldwide.

Moreover, the record of Soviet efforts in the Third World is not brilliant. If today it enjoys significant influence in such relatively unimportant countries as Angola, Mozambique, Cuba, Ethiopia, Afghanistan, and South Yemen, it has also lost ground in such important and populous countries as China, Indonesia, Egypt, and Somalia. The Soviet Union lacks the economic means of the United States that would allow it to establish a stable and enduring influence far from its borders. Besides, those states that turn to the Soviets for aid are generally headed by nationalist regimes seeking to defend themselves from Western imperialism. They are not about to let themselves fall easily under the domination of another great power.

It is also worth noting that the selective aid that the Soviet Union gives to revolutionary movements in the Third World has less to do with internationalist solidarity than with Soviet state interests: Every revolution provokes a U.S. reaction that naturally pushes it towards the Soviet Union, which, for its part, cannot help but welcome any diminution in the sphere of influence of its main adversary. The limits of communist solidarity were shown clearly in 1972 during Nixon's visit to Moscow. This first visit of a U.S. president to the USSR, the high point of the era of detente, took place less than a month after the mining of the port of Haiphong and the North Vietnamese coast and the escalation of the bombing of that country, which was, after all, a member in good standing of the so-called socialist camp.

Even this brief sketch of the history of Soviet foreign policy suggests that the arguments advanced by NATO spokespersons to prove there is a Soviet threat do not hold up to serious scrutiny. It is probably easier to argue that the more immediate threat to the freedom and independence of the peoples that inhabit Canada comes from their own state and from their neighbour to the south.

The New Cold War

The Cold War that followed World War II was also based upon the notion of a Soviet threat. At the time, the spectre of an expansionist Soviet state, with an army unequalled in a prostrate and defenceless Europe, was used to justify the formal reversal of the wartime alliances, the creation of the Atlantic Alliance, and the rearmament of Germany.

But the reality was very different. Soviet Russia, with its 20 million dead and uncounted invalids, was neither physically nor morally capable of launching a large-scale foreign invasion. At best it could have waged war for its survival. The most populous and developed parts of the country were in ruins, with some 25 million people without permanent shelter there at the end of the war.

On the other hand, in the United States no bombs had fallen and human losses had been relatively limited. The United States had more than doubled its productive capacity during the war and had, for a time, a monopoly on the atomic bomb and on long-range bombers. Moreover, between 1945 and 1948, the Soviet Union reduced its army from 11.5 million to less than 3 million soldiers. The remobilization occurred only after the proclamation of the Truman Doctrine, which pledged the United States to fight communism and revolution across the globe. Even so, it took the Soviet Union four more years to again reach the five million figure.

As the historian Isaac Deutscher stated, the world had never known so gigantic and so unreal a war scare as the one that justified the creation of NATO and the rearming of Germany.[7] There were a number of major reasons behind the alarm:

1. For the Western States, the Grand Alliance of 1941-45 with the USSR had never been more than a marriage of convenience dictated by the necessity of defeating the axis powers. This alliance had been preceded by a quarter century of mistrust and hostility towards the Soviet Union (especially on the part of the United States), which began from the very first days of the October Revolution. Therefore, once victory had been won the alliance lost its raison d'être. What is more, in the interval, the former pariah state had become a great power and demanded to be recognized as such.

2. World War II, like the Great War, had revolutionary consequences, especially in the Third World. And even if the Soviet Union was not at the origin of this agitation (on the contrary, it preached moderation everywhere), anti-Sovietism and anti-Communism were very efficient means of modifying public opinion in the developed capitalist countries

in favour of counter-revolutionary interventions abroad as well as repression of the increasingly restive labour movement and dissident intellectuals at home.

3. Finally, the claimed Soviet threat helped to cement the cohesion of the developed capitalist states around the United States, which at this time established its economic and political hegemony in the capitalist world.

All these factors, in one way or another, play a role today in the new Cold War. Like the first, this one followed upon a brief period of good relations and co-operation between the West and the Soviet Union. Detente was only the second such period in East-West relations, and especially Soviet-U.S. relations. During detente, as in the Grand Alliance, it seemed as though the historic aspiration of the Soviet Union was at last on its way to realization: The Soviet Union seemed to be winning recognition by the West as a legitimate great power with which dialogue and mutually beneficial trade were not only possible, but necessary.

If the Grand Alliance had been based on the necessity of defeating the fascist power, detente, for its part, was based on the fact that the Soviet Union, at the cost of great effort expended in the 1960s, had finally reached nuclear parity with the United States. It was relative parity, since the United States still enjoyed a large technical and numerical advantage, but now each side possessed enough bombs and delivery systems so that even in the case of a surprise attack, the other would have enough destructive power to inflict unacceptable losses on the attacker. Mutual assured destruction—MAD—had become a reality. In Kissinger's own words: "For most of the post-war period, the Soviet Union had been virtually defenceless against an American first strike. Nor could it improve its position significantly by attacking, since our counterblow would have posed unacceptable risks." However, by the end of the 1960s the Soviet Union's arsenal had reached the point where, in an exchange, U.S. casualties would have run into the millions. "To pretend that such a prospect would not affect American readiness to resort to nuclear weapons would have been an evasion of our responsibilities," said Kissinger.[8]

Again, many factors contributed to the collapse of detente. But what is striking are the parallels with the causes of the first Cold War. To begin with, the parity reached in the late 1960s was only relative. For its part, the United States had no intention of renouncing its lead (even if logically one can wonder what this nuclear superiority is worth in practice, at least in purely military terms). Thus the first funds for the development of the Cruise missile were allocated in 1973, only a few months after the signing of the SALT I Treaty on the limitation of strategic arms. For its part, the Soviet Union, while respecting the signed accords, continued to pursue its arms program so that the numerical gap gradually narrowed, although technologically it remains five to seven years behind the United States.

This development disappointed U.S. ruling circles. Even the most moderate elements found it hard to accept that the United States would cease to be the most powerful nation in the world, and that its great ideological enemy was protected from attack.

According to the American conception of detente, in exchange for good relations with the United States the Soviet Union was supposed to show moderation in other parts of the world. It was supposed to help hold back revolutionary and radical nationalist movements. This was Kissinger's and Nixon's concept of "linkage". However, around 1974 a new wave of revolutionary upheaval began: Angola, Mozambique, Ethiopia, Iran, Afghanistan, Nicaragua, El Salvador. Even if the Soviet Union played no role in the outbreak of the movements, which all had deep domestic roots, in the cases of Vietnam, Afghanistan, and Angola, at least, it furnished, directly or indirectly, significant military aid. And even where there was no aid, the new strategic potential of the Soviet Union had a certain moderating influence on the U.S. will to intervene, as, for example, in Iran. At the same time, the rise of OPEC highlighted Western dependence on Third World resources.

Again, it was useful for the U.S. administration to see the hand of Moscow in all these developments. Just as after World War II, this was to make easier the mobilization of public opinion (still suffering, we were told, from the cursed "Vietnam syndrome") in favour of foreign intervention and enormous expenditures on conventional weapons destined for use in the Third World. (These expenditures are by far the largest part of Western military budgets.)

Finally, the new Cold War, the heightened East-West tension, is a way of applying pressure by the United States on the other developed capitalist countries. The United States feared that detente, and especially the substantial trade between West Germany and the Soviet bloc, was weakening the commitment of the Western European countries to the Atlantic Alliance. The fear of war helps to cement this alliance. In the economic sphere, the United States, whose relative situation seriously declined after the 1950s, wanted to encourage trade concessions from Japan and Western Europe and to push them to increase their own military budgets.

It should be emphasized that the new Cold War launched by NATO was not a response to any radical changes in Soviet behaviour, which remained quite constant. According to the CIA's and NATO's own estimates, the annual rate of growth in real terms of the Soviet military budget actually declined after 1976 (the beginning of the end of detente) from 4 to 5 per cent to 2 per cent.[9]

As for the issue of the arms themselves—the issue that so monopolizes media attention—suffice it to say that U.S. technological superiority is universally recognized. The Soviet Union still has nothing as advanced as the U.S. Cruise and Pershing missiles, though it is sure to have them soon.[10] Averill Harriman, former U.S. ambassador to the Soviet Union and advisor to U.S. presidents, stated in January 1984 that "The Soviet leaders want serious negotiations," while Reagan approached the talks on intermediate and long-range missiles "as a propaganda forum, an occasion to hurl invectives, as a mask to cover the new deployment of arms, an arena in which to gain advantage, rather than a path that should lead to the survival of mankind on this planet".[11] George Kenan, the noted author of "containment" and also a former ambassador to the Soviet Union and presidential advisor, maintains that each new stage in the arms race has been initiated by the United States.[12]

It is interesting to follow the evolution of the justification offered for the Star Wars program. When it was first announced to Congress, it was a means to rid the world, once and for all, of the threat of nuclear weapons. It mattered little to Reagan that this task could be approached infinitely more rationally and cheaply by reaching an agreement with the Soviets to dismantle existing nuclear weaponry. But when scepticism and opposition to this truly fantastic Star Wars initiative grew too strong, the old reliable, the ultimate justification, was paraded out: The Russians started and they are far ahead. "The Russians drove us to it," former National Security Advisor McFarlane told the public on the eve of the Geneva summit in November 1985. Gone was the desire to rid the world of nuclear weapons. In fact, the Star Wars program, at least as far as the U.S. military is concerned, is aimed at restoring U.S. nuclear predominance by giving it a new first strike capacity,[13] and that is why it is non-negotiable.

Soviet Responsibility and the Peace Movement

There is a current in the peace movement that argues that the Soviet Union bears no responsibility for the arms race, that its policies in this area are legitimately defensive, that the Soviets have no choice. This current is mainly, though not exclusively, to be found in the peace councils controlled by the communist parties. In the Soviet-bloc countries they are the official, state-supported peace movements.

The analysis presented above does, in fact, support the idea that the Soviets have an essentially defensive conception of their role in the East-

West confrontation. But unlike the peace councils, the non-aligned peace movement considers this conception of defence illegitimate and harmful. After all, the motivation behind the Soviet domination of Eastern Europe is equally defensive. But it remains illegitimate to base the security of a state, no matter how powerful, on the deprivation of the rights and freedoms of other peoples.

The same judgement must apply to the Soviet policy in the arms race. Regardless of how defensive the motivation of the Soviet leaders might be, they promise to vaporize the population of the Western states if their country suffers a nuclear attack on their part. For ordinary people, the distinction between defensive and offensive nuclear weapons is totally meaningless. They cannot help but see in the Soviet arsenal pointed at their heads, a threat to their fundamental right to life, and a life free from terror.

It is for this reason, above all, that Soviet efforts to woo the Western peace movement have such little credibility. (This is not necessarily to question the sincerity of recent Soviet proposals for a mutual deep reduction of the arsenals or to freeze nuclear testing.)

The real Soviet threat does not come from any claimed aggressive designs on the West, but from the very conception of security held by the Soviet regime, a conception that seeks to guarantee the security of the state on the basis of its military power and of accords pursued with the United States. Since the latter is not prepared to give up its quest for superiority and since the Soviet Union insists on parity, it becomes obvious that negotiations in themselves are not a path that can lead to real results. This is the sad conclusion one is forced to draw from the past 20 years of East-West talks and accords. Thus, the Soviet arms policy remains the mirror image of the U.S. (with a certain technological lag) and continues to furnish NATO with its best justification for a policy of escalation.

One can ask if the Soviet Union really has a choice. But an alternative does exist. Instead of giving priority to the pursuit of agreements with the Western states, the Soviet leadership could seek honest accords with the forces fighting for disarmament in the West. But such honest accords have to be based on real—unilateral—measures that aim at reducing the nuclear threat directed at the peoples of the West. For example, the Soviet Union could begin unilaterally to dismantle its nuclear arsenal (starting with the SS-20s) and invite representatives and experts from the peace movement to inspect this. Such a policy could no longer be portrayed by NATO as propaganda and it would give the peace movement in the West a boost such that the governments in Europe, and eventually even North America, could not long resist its pressure.

Moreover, the Soviet Union could take such measures without exposing itself to any real military danger, since in the crazy logic of nuclear arms, a hundred missiles are as threatening as a thousand, despite what the Soviet and U.S. leaders claim. Even with its nuclear arsenal drastically reduced, the Soviet Union, in case of a Western attack, would still be able to inflict unacceptable damage on the enemy.

In theory the bureaucratic regime in the USSR could adopt such a genuinely internationalist policy. But in reality it is doubtful that it could change a foreign policy orientation that corresponds so well to the interests and the ethos of those who rule the country—an orientation which, at the time it was adopted over 50 years ago, coincided with the consolidation of bureaucratic power. After all, a regime that distrusts its own people to the point where it feels it must crush any independent initiative from below is hardly likely to decide to tie its security to popular movements abroad that it cannot control.

One must conclude that neither the USSR nor the United States has the will or the interest to break the logic of the arms race. The idea of "multilateral disarmament through negotiations among states", a strategy pushed by the Soviet Union and the peace councils, can lead only to paralysis of the peace movement. A strategy that combines unilateralism and non-alignment—which includes support for the independent peace movement in the East and for the right to organize freely to oppose state policy—is the only one that has a chance to succeed, because it corresponds to a realistic analysis of the respective roles of the United States and the Soviet Union in the arms race.

Notes

1. N. Chomsky et al., *Superpowers in Collision* (Harmondsworth, 1982), p. 46.

2. For an analysis of this aspect of Soviet policy, see F. Claudin, *The Communist Movement* (New York and London, 1975); and P. Frank, *Histoire de l'Internationale communiste* (Paris, 1979).

3. For a history and analysis of Soviet foreign policy after World War II, see J. Lévesque, *L'U.R.S.S. et sa politique internationale* (Paris, 1980), parts 3-6; for the Brezhnev period in particular, see R. Edmonds, *Soviet Foreign Policy: The Brezhnev Years* (New York, 1983).

4. J. Vanous, "East European Slowdown," *Problems of Communism*, vol. 31 (July-August 1982), p. 6.

5. See J. Steele, *Socialism with a German Face* (London, 1977), chaps. 3 and 4, especially pp. 70-71.

6. G. Prins, ed., *Defended to Death* (Harmondsworth, 1983), p. 200. See also F. Halliday, *Threat from the East?* (Harmondsworth, 1982).

7. I. Deutscher, *Ironies of History*, (Berkeley, 1971), pp. 150-151.

8. H. Kissinger, *White House Years* (New York, 1979), pp. 83-84.

9. "L'effort soviétique ralentirait," *Le Devoir* (Montreal), 19 September 1983; "L'effort militaire soviétique dimune," *Le Devoir*, 31 January 1984.

10. See for example, the interview with G. Kistiakowsky, former science advisor to President Eisenhower, in E.P. Thompson and D. Smith, eds., *Protest and Survive* (New York and London, 1981), pp. 126-127.

11. *New York Times*, 2 and 3 January 1984.

12. G. Kenan, *The Nuclear Delusion* (New York, 1982).

13. E.P. Thompson and Dan Thompson, *Star Wars-Self-Destruct Inc.* (London, 1985).

Non-Alignment and Detente from Below

Ronald Babin, Eric Shragge, and Jean-François Beaudet

IN RECENT YEARS many in the Canadian disarmament movement have become concerned about the political repression of participants in unofficial peace groups in Eastern Europe. This concern sharpened with the imprisonment of Russian activists Alexander Shatravka and Vladimir Brodsky of the Group to Establish Trust between the U.S. and the USSR. This case stimulated a broad debate within the Canadian movement on the importance of building effective links with the independent groups working for peace in the Eastern bloc.[1]

The debate and concern in Canada is part of the development of a broad peace movement that crosses international borders and blocs. It is based on a political vision embodied in the concepts of non-alignment and detente from below. These concepts are increasingly shaping the reflections and actions of the movements, East and West, that are attempting to lay the foundations for a real and durable peace, a peace not based on a balance of terror and the force of arms.

Seen from this perspective, the struggle for peace from below represents the activation of those who are not represented or who have been kept in a position of subordination. In addition, non-alignment is an invitation to escape from an imperial-type system of domination made up of two rival hegemonic systems that are mutually reinforcing in their dynamics and militaristic rationalizations. Under these circumstances, it is not pure neutralism or the absence of a position, but more the affirmation of a growing will to address the serious problems related to the division of the world into two spheres of influence according to the bipolar logic of the blocs.

In conjunction with the development of a non-aligned peace movement, we are seeing an increasing consciousness of our common responsibility for the survival of humanity. This responsibility seems to increase with the unrestrained development of deadly weapons and an apparently unending arms race between the United States and the USSR. The idea of non-alignment gives us the option of not expressing a preference for either of the superpowers and consequently not getting bogged down in sterile debates apportioning blame. It works to build a broad transnational movement for disarmament which goes beyond ideological blocs and national barriers.

In this sense the new antiwar movement shows a desire to keep its distance from the superpowers and their allies; it no longer counts on bilateral and multilateral negotiations among states as the only means to disarmament and peace. The movement refuses to give a carte blanche to the logic of the state, opting rather to put the emphasis on the direct and democratic involvement of the people. It is a choice in favour of developing independent involvement at the base of society, which in turn may have a positive influence on the official policies of governments.

Different Possibilities for Dialogue

Through this kind of people's diplomacy there is an attempt to initiate the actual practice of detente from below. The significance of this orientation can be seen in the progress already made towards one of its major objectives, the establishment of an alternative dialogue between the populations in the West and the East. From the start, the main question and point of conflict has been with whom and how to conduct this dialogue. With what groups or movements should these transnational alliances be built? This question is not simple, because the Western peace movements quickly realized that there were two possibilities for dialogue.

In the first place, there are the peace committees and peace councils that developed in Eastern Europe in the years following World War II and which presently constitute a huge peace bureaucracy. Most of the time these organizations act as a pipeline for Soviet positions in the area of foreign policy. They are joined by national and regional branches (such as the Canadian Peace Council and Quebec Peace Council) to make up the World Peace Council, which was formed around the Stockholm Appeal of 1948 and later established its headquarters in Helsinki, Finland.

Secondly, a more recent possibility has developed through voices demanding, in a more or less organized way, the right of protest in the countries of Eastern Europe. Solidarnosc in Poland and Charter 77 in Czechoslovakia are examples of efforts to bring about social change and defend civil rights. In addition there are also new groups formed outside of official structures to raise the issue of disarmament. This is the case in East Germany, with groups of conscientious objectors and women's and youth groups for disarmament; in Hungary, with the Dialogue Movement and the Indigo organization of artists for peace; and in the USSR itself, with the Groups to Establish Trust between the United States and the USSR, as well as youth groups that have taken the name Independent Initiative.

The non-aligned peace movement of the West understands that it has more in common with the independent groups than with the official committees of the East. In fact, it is possible to see in the independent actions of the groups and movements of the East an effort to bring about greater citizen involvement, often through the use of innovative methods resembling those used by the social movements of the West. A connection becomes evident because on both sides action is motivated by efforts to change an explosive and oppressive status quo. Although they are expressed differently, there are more similarities in the concerns in the East and the West than in the differences separating them.

This is not the case with the Peace Councils, which take general positions in favour of peace but also avoid important issues. The question of nuclear energy is a revealing example. Most of the Peace Councils support development of nuclear energy and invoke the official argument that makes a false distinction between civilian and military nuclear technology. This truncated version of the facts helps conceal the overlap of the two and the vertical and horizontal proliferation of nuclear weapons as a consequence of civilian nuclear technology.

The orientations of the Peace Councils are often defined by their organizational links with the structures of Soviet power. Their actions are most often dictated by Soviet objectives, particularly its desire to achieve military parity with the United States and recognition as an equal player in world politics. The means to do this is through official negotiations between states. But the unending negotiations between the United States and the Soviet Union have produced very limited results on disarmament. Thus the orientation of the peace councils ends up being a defence of the status quo.

This status quo is a system where two rival superpowers manage the continuous conflict of an arms race which, although extremely dangerous, is mutually advantageous in terms of the exercise of power over others. Thus the peace councils tend to support mutual recognition and multi- or bilateral talks as the means to achieve arms control.

Solidarity West to East

Such realizations help to put in perspective the particular importance given to rapprochement with groups and movements independent of official structures and which are struggling for peace and human rights in Eastern Europe. Since the early 1980s there has been a movement in this direction initiated by many European groups. The movement continues to develop new ideas and to broaden to include groups in the West (including some in North America) and in the East (especially Solidarnosc). A review of these developments allows us to identify three successive stages and helps us better to understand the meaning and significance of this movement.

The rapprochement took root when the groups in the West learned of the existence of independent groups and their activities for peace in the East. For example, on January 25, 1982, the Berlin Appeal for the demilitarization of East Germany was launched by the Protestant pastor Reiner Appelman. A few weeks later, on February 13, the city of Dresden was the site of an unauthorized gathering of five thousand young people at a peace conference organized by the Protestant churches on the anniversary of the bombing of the city during the Second World War.[2] In Moscow, the Group to Establish Trust between the U.S. and the USSR was established on June 4. This group, which later spread to other Soviet cities, was founded by Sergei Batovrin and ten other people. A year later, in March 1983, news came from Hungary of the participation of the independent Dialogue Movement in a demonstration organized by the official Hungarian Peace Council. The Dialogue Movement used its own slogans and attracted several hundred people to its banner.

However, there was also news of repression and exemplary persecution of several individuals aimed at discouraging independent peace activities. Many groups in the West began to act, at first with numerous expressions of support for those being mistreated. For example, the August 1982 arrest of Sergei Batovrin and his subsequent incarceration in a psychiatric hospital brought a world-wide appeal for his release. After only one month the Amnesty International campaign brought his release. Subsequently, various methods have been used, including candlelight vigils in front of Soviet embassies and consulates and letter-writing campaigns protesting the arrest of various individuals, including Oleg Radzinski of Independent Initiative in April 1983 and Ladislav Lis of Charter 77 in March 1984.

In several cities major demonstrations in 1982, 1983, and 1984 took the form of human chains between the embassies of the United States and the Soviet Union. This was to express opposition to the arms race carried on by the two superpowers and also to symbolize the solidarity and the growing links with the independent groups in the East. This was the case in

Montreal, for example, in October 1983 and 1984. To develop further these appeals for solidarity, direct contact was established with activists expelled from the Eastern bloc countries, such as the 20 young East German pacifists exiled to West Germany in June 1983. One of them, Roland Jahn, immediately expressed his desire to return home and continue his work for peace, asking for the assistance of the West German government and the United Nations to do so. There were also expressions of support during trips by individuals and groups to East bloc countries. In 1983, European Nuclear Disarmament (END) in London put out an important series of publications on the independent groups of Hungary, the USSR, East Germany, Czechoslovakia, and Turkey.[3]

All this made clear the progress in developing the important links between the independent groups and movements of the East and West.

Across the Frontiers

The END Special Reports marked the beginning of a second phase of contact, one of shared reflection, exchange of information, and public dialogue. This phase, symbolized by the circulation of open letters between independent groups of East and West, saw the exchange of points of view on a variety of issues. Many of these documents were published in magazines such as *END Journal* and *Bulletin du CODENE*. In addition, three new magazines were launched in the United States in 1984 to disseminate this information in North America: *Peace and Democracy News*, *Across Frontiers: For Solidarity East and West*, and *Return Address: Moscow—International News Bulletin on Independent Peace Activity in the USSR*.[4] In Quebec, a special issue of the *Revue internationale d'action communautaire* drew attention to this development by publishing an article and some open letters between Charter 77 and END.[5]

All of this activity emphasized the importance given to understanding the significant differences between the ways of life and the perceptions of problems in East and West. For those in the West it was necessary to act quickly to reverse the arms race and eliminate the danger of nuclear war. For those in the East this issue could not be separated from the struggle for human rights and freedoms. Thus, at the outset, there was no agreement on the nature of the problems and the urgency with which they needed to be addressed.

Yet in spite of this it is not difficult to see that the two approaches are more complementary than they are different; that linking them allows us to develop a larger perspective embracing both "sides". In fact, the East's vision, focusing on the domestic policies of those countries, helps us to recognize the importance of domestic social and political relations. The West's vision, more centred on international politics, helps give a broader dimension to the analysis in the East on a whole range of mechanisms of domination in the world.

In brief, this rapprochement promoted a broad learning process where both sides got to know each other better and learn from our differences. It was through this exchange that both sides could recognize the existence of common interests. The notion of detente from below sought to strengthen this process. A common analysis began to emerge, particularly with regard to the European situation. The image of Europe was that of a continent occupied militarily in the East and politically and psychologically in the West. Thus, the struggle for peace and freedom implies not only the removal of nuclear weapons on both sides and respect for human rights in the East bloc countries, but also a total redefinition of European relations and politics in order to go beyond antagonisms and the categories of the Cold War.

Towards an Alternative Vision

The alternative vision of a free and peaceful Europe advanced in 1984 in discussion papers and statements of principle. It can be found, notably, in the working paper, "European Declaration of Peace", prepared by END for the Third Convention on Nuclear Disarmament in Europe held in Perugia, Italy, in July. "We look forward," said the Declaration,

> to a Europe, not of uniformity but of diversity, in which there are many differences in political and social systems. As the shadows of superpower domination and of nuclear threat are removed from our continent, so individual nations will gain greater autonomy and the freedom to determine their own political and social systems and foreign policies according to their own democratic choice.

The desire to change European political realities was echoed in an open letter written by Charter 77 of Czechoslovakia to the participants of the Perugia Convention:

> The only way out of the blind alley into which the policy of military might has driven Europe is to express principled opposition to this policy and to formulate instead a policy to genuinely unite all those opposed to the nuclear madness in a mighty democratic coalition expressing the authentic wishes of the inhabitants of Europe. Today's woeful situation would not be possible were the people of Europe not divided 'internally' both

ideologically and politically. This internal division is the basis for the 'external' division of Europe, its geopolitical division, and not the contrary. Our view of the spiritual basis for a policy capable of achieving the broadest possible alliance of democratic and peace forces and hence of breaching the surviving Cold War structures, may be summed up as a desire to overcome this division and move towards a new internal unity, one inspired by democratic and moral strength.[6]

The decision to issue these statements at the Perugia convention shows the importance placed on these annual four-day meetings. From the first meeting in 1982, one to two thousand people (mainly Europeans, but some from North America and the Pacific) have gathered each year for intense discussion and exploration of alternatives for the future. And with each year more progress is made on East-West issues. These issues were raised with some reticence in Brussels in 1982, with some caution in Berlin in 1983, but with enthusiasm in Amsterdam in 1985. The Perugia convention was the turning point that warrants attention.

Before Perugia, East-West questions were approached cautiously so as not to break completely with the peace councils, which at that time were seen as a good means of transmitting to the USSR the various points of view developing in the peace movements in the West. In particular, it was hoped to persuade the Soviet authorities to accept as legitimate the independent peace movements in the East in spite of the difference between their approaches and those of the official councils and committees. The Perugia convention continued in this hope, trying to bring together for the first time in the same forum delegates from the movements in the West, the peace committees and councils in the East, and the independent groups in the East. For the first time, the official committees were invited as full participants in the hope that there would emerge from the tripartite exchange the recognition of independent peace groups in the East and an end to their repression. Out of a total of 1,200 delegates, 100 were from the Soviet Committee for the Defence of Peace, and the peace councils of Eastern Europe and various countries around the world. It did not include the 59 independent delegates from the East who had been prevented from leaving their countries. Their forced absence led to a major protest during the opening session and coloured the rest of the convention with a climate of confrontation.

Conference in Berlin

Thus began a new, third, phase of the East-West reflection, one focused on the notions of non-alignment and detente from below. The conference gave birth to the European Network for an East-West Dialogue, whose first task was to organize a discussion forum to take a deeper look at this political and strategic debate. In early February 1985, West Berlin was the site of a conference titled "Peace in a Divided Europe, Forty Years After Yalta." This meeting brought together 200 people: representatives of the peace movements in the West and, from the East, representatives of the movements for social and political freedom as well as the independent peace groups. The participants evaluated the state of a Europe still divided 40 years after Yalta, discussed a post-Yalta future, and encouraged the creation of more formal East-West links among those challenging the blocs.

Above all, the meeting allowed a frank and direct exchange of views among activists from West and East whose points of view are sometimes very different. It also provided a unique opportunity for direct meetings among the various opposition groups from the Eastern bloc. Exiled representatives of Solidarnosc were able to meet members of the independent peace groups of Hungary and East Germany as well as representatives of Charter 77 to discuss different possibilities for uniting their efforts and creating links. They also explored various possibilities for co-operation with the peace movement of the West.

Discussion in the workshops revealed many errors of judgement on both sides. For example, Solidarnosc criticized the Western peace movement for failing to react vigorously enough to the declaration of martial law in Poland on December 13, 1981. Mary Kaldor, a representative of END, admitted this had probably been one of their most serious mistakes. On the other hand, a member of the West German Green Party criticized the members of Solidarnosc for sometimes considering Reagan an ally. In turn, a member of Solidarnosc said that an effort was being made in certain Polish circles to become more critical of the Reagan government. (Solidarnosc has expressed solidarity with social and political struggles in the Third World, such as that of Chilean unionists.)

The conference was also an opportunity for reflection on the mechanisms that maintain the Cold War. For example, a Czech who had participated in the resistance to the invasion of Warsaw Pact troops in 1968 described how the invasion had been used first by Western governments to justify their increasing militarization and secondly by Eastern governments to justify the political status quo in their bloc. In fact, Czechoslovakian "socialism with a human face" had proven to be a third path which was just as threatening to the capitalist system as the "true socialism" of the Eastern bloc. In a similar vein, Mary Kaldor recalled that the deployment of U.S. Pershing II missiles was used by the Soviets as a pretext to justify the subsequent repression of the independent peace and social change movements in Eastern Europe.

The militarization of the West and the suppression of freedom and human rights in the East are two facets of a single system of power and domination within which each side needs the other to justify itself. Most of those present agreed that it was necessary to go beyond Yalta and the present division of the world into blocs. Rather than simply the elimination of nuclear weapons from Europe, as proposed by some from the West, those from the East spoke of the demilitarization of Europe. The stability of the bloc system was widely questioned; the only stability offered by this division is that of repression and the march towards the extermination of humanity.

Throughout the conference, one thing was especially clear: the participants now saw themselves as partners in a new type of open East-West dialogue and not as pawns playing the game of either Moscow or Washington. Recorded messages from Jacek Kuron of Solidarnosc and Jaroslav Sabata of Charter 77 demonstrated the confidence that Polish and Czech intellectuals now have in the Western peace movement in spite of certain disagreements with Western activists (such as the call for unilateral disarmament in the West).

New Initiatives From Below

In the months following the Berlin conference there were many initiatives:
- In February 1985 Moscow saw the start of a process of "kitchen table diplomacy" parallel to the Geneva talks. The first meeting brought together citizens of Denmark, England, Finland, and the Soviet Union.
- On International Women's Day, March 8, 1985, women from the five countries where new nuclear missiles had just been deployed (Czechoslovakia, East Germany, Italy, West Germany, and Great Britain) issued an open letter to all Europeans appealing for local initiatives from below as a means of working towards a nuclear-free Europe. (See box.)
- In March, Charter 77 issued the *Prague Appeal*, which proposed action aimed beyond the logic of the blocs. The appeal stimulated intense discussion at the Fourth END Convention in Amsterdam. The appeal suggested that the Helsinki Accords (of the conference on Security and Co-operation in Europe) serve as a basis for future action. The second meeting of the European Network for an East-West Dialogue, held in Milan in May 1986, furthered the reflection in this direction.
- During the summer of 1985, an international network sprang up to express solidarity with the Moscow Trust Group. This was followed in November by an appeal for the formation of an Urgent Action Network

to provide ongoing solidarity and the circulation of news about the Soviet Trust Groups. The network has been particularly active in raising concern over the Shatravka and Brodsky imprisonments. More recently it has also become increasingly involved in issues relating to the jailing of Trust Group activist Larissa Chukaeva. Not only has she been put into prison but she has also been determined an "unfit mother" and had her three-year-old child taken away as a ward of the court. The Urgent Action Network wishes to raise this disquieting new development, clearly evidence of an escalation of repression facing independent peace activists.

Problems and Promise

Detente from below assumes real peace to be a process that begins with a solidarity between people as a means of pushing the state system. Peace groups in the West, faced with charges that they are dupes of the USSR, can point to their practice of detente from below and to their support of independent peace activists. Non-alignment implies more than a critique of foreign policy and of military questions. It implies bringing together the peoples and movements on both sides, who seek peace not only through the reduction of militarism but also through a redefinition of political life.

There are obvious problems with this process. The peace groups in Eastern bloc countries face harassment and repression for even the most moderate activities, keeping these groups small and vulnerable. With the exception of certain events, particularly in the GDR, they lack a mass following such as Solidarnosc developed. Western peace activists have to be realistic about the difficulties of, and the courage necessary for, independent peace activists in the East. Support for their efforts is obviously an important activity, but in the short term it is unlikely that these groups, particularly in the Soviet Union, Hungary, and Czechoslovakia, will become mass movements. Furthermore, in the West, those engaged in support activities for these groups must be careful to avoid the traps of the Cold War.

In order to overcome the false polarization of lack of freedom in the East and of total liberty in the West, the Canadian disarmament movement needs to speak out strongly against the repression of peace activists in the West: of those in Turkey, of peace camps in Camiso, Italy, and Greenham Common, England, and of the arrests of activists such as 40 people in Montreal who had participated in the International Shadow Project marking the fortieth anniversary of the Hiroshima bombing on August 6, 1985. The issues of peace and freedom are not as clearly cut on

For Detente from Below, for the Denuclearization of Europe: An open letter by women from East and West to all citizens of Europe

We are women in five European countries where the deployment of new American and Soviet weapons has begun. We are women from different cultures, from Eastern and Western, Northern and Southern Europe, some of us involved in the church, others not, some of us feminists, pacifists and members of many other human rights and environmental movements.

Despite our differences, we are united by the will for self-determination, to struggle against the culture of militarism in the world, against uniforms and violence, against our children being educated as soldiers and against the senseless waste of resources. We demand the right of self-determination for all individuals and peoples. We want to make a specific cultural contribution to changing existing social structures. That is why we also challenge conventional gender roles and why we ask men to do the same.

The freedom to determine one's own fate also means freedom from exploitation and violence: in our thoughts and actions, at our places of work, in our relationship to nature and the relationship between men and women, between generations, between states, between East and West and between North and South in global terms.

Together we want to break this circle of violence and the anxieties created in us by this violence: anxiety about nuclear weapons, fearing the death of humanity and the end of the earth, fears about the rape of our bodies and souls. Together we wish to confront these anxieties and be able to overcome them, no longer illegally, but with the right to free expression of opinion for everyone, especially in those places where the right is denied on a daily basis. There can be no realistic peace perspective without respect for human rights.

The deployment of new nuclear weapons in our countries has limited our freedom and increased our fears. Our obligation to break the circle of violence has grown because of our potential shared responsibility for a possible catastrophe. We are conscious of being both perpetrators and victims of systems of violence. In both roles, we are not the ones who have made the decisions. We reject both roles.

Nor are we reassured by the fact that representatives of both super-powers are about to negotiate over our heads again in Geneva. Once again we are expected to pin our hopes on their seeing reason and voluntarily renouncing the production and use of weapons of mass destruction. Once again talks on how to hold talks are supposed to make us believe that it is possible to solve the problems from above.

Instead of this, we choose the way of self-determined initiatives from below. This road does not go via the militarization of society, which is why we reject any involvement in the preparations for war—nor does it go via traverse missile ramps or the destruction of nature and interpersonal relationships.

We do not want a peace which oppresses us, nor a war which will annihilate us.

Forty years after Auschwitz and Hiroshima, forty years after the bloc confrontation began, we want now, at last, to begin collectively getting to know and understand each other better and meet one another beyond the wall which divides not merely the borders of our countries but all too often our hearts and minds as well.

We have begun detente from below: Join us!

This statement has been signed by women from all five missile deployment countries: United Kingdom, German Democratic Republic, Federal Republic of Germany, Italy, and Czechoslovakia.

8 March 1985

---

an East-West axis as some would suggest. By linking them, the disarmament and peace movement raises the important option of non-alignment and of de-alignment from those who disseminate such a world view.

In Canada, the activities of detente from below have remained at the level of support for individual activists and of visits by Canadians to Eastern bloc countries. As a country geographically situated between the superpowers, Canada could play a stronger political role if it were to move in the direction of non-alignment. For this to occur, the permanent enemy hypothesis—the USSR as the main adversary—has to be challenged. This approach has been the main justification of Canada's support for NATO and for U.S. policy. Further, a nation remains an enemy so long as its people can be presented as inherently different or as sharing goals in direct conflict to ours. In order to undermine this assumption and the official image of the enemy, detente from below shows the common interest of individuals and groups for peace in ways that leaders refuse. Detente from below challenges the basis of the Cold War by showing that people share a common stake in eliminating the arms race. There are ways of doing this that initially have to proceed through official channels. Twinning of schools, communities, and cities, and supporting exchanges can have the effect of debunking the permanent enemy hypothesis and of developing common experiences between people.

Progress towards disarmament and peace will be made as people develop a common view that security will result not from more arms and "deterrence" but rather from more disarmament, more freedom, and more justice. Detente from below represents a new vision of peace between peoples. It is a vision that undermines the assumptions of the Cold War.

Notes

1. The development of a support network (the Urgent Action Network) for the USSR Trust groups has been encouraged by groups such as Act for Disarmament in Toronto and the Coalition québecoise pour le Désarmement et la paix (CQDP). Volume 1, Number 11 of *Peace Magazine* has included a comprehensive look by. John Bacher at the various independent movements working for peace in Eastern Europe. At the 1985 general meeting of the Physicians for Nuclear Responsibility, an impassioned debate broke out on the merits and advisability of their giving formal support to cardiologist and peace activist, Vladimir Brodsky.

2. This activity was held in a church that had a capacity of around one thousand people. Three thousand people managed to gather inside, with two thousand outside. The gathering could have been much larger had not the East German authorities delayed some of the trains carrying many more supporters to this independent peace initiative.

3. Ferenc Koszegi and E.P. Thompson, *The New Hungarian Peace Movement* (London, END Special Report, 1983), p. 54; Jean Stead and Danielle Grunberg, *Moscow Independent Peace Group* (London, END Special Report, 1982); John Sandford, *The Sword and the Ploughshare. Autonomous Peace Initiatives in East Germany* (London, END Special Report, 1983), p. 111; Jan Kavan and Zdena Tomin, *Voices from Prague. Documents on Czechoslovakia and the Peace Movement* (London, END and Palach Press Limited, 1983), p. 75; Jean Furtado, ed., *Turkey: Peace on Trial* (London, END Publications and Merlin, 1983).

4. *Peace and Democracy News*, Bulletin of the Campaign for Peace and Democracy East and West, P.O. Box 1640, Cathedral Station, New York, NY, USA, 10025; *Across Frontiers*, P.O. Box 2382, Berkeley, CA, USA, 94702; *Return Address: Moscow*, P.O. Box 1073, New York, NY, USA, 10040.

5. "Le Mouvement pour le Désarmement et la Paix", *Revue internationale d'Action communautaire/International Review of Community Development*, no. 12/52, Autumn 1984. Co-edited by Jean-Guy Vaillancourt and Ronald Babin. Montreal, RIAC/IRCD, Ecole de service social, Université de Montréal.

6. This open letter has been published among other places in *Across Frontiers*, vol. 1, no. 3-4, Winter-Spring 1985, p. 11.

Part Two

Organizing for Peace

A Feminist Approach to Militarism and Peace

Phyllis Aronoff

Comiso, Italy, March 1983: In four days of activities women protest both the deployment of nuclear weapons at the nearby American military base and sexual violence against women.[1]

Cole Bay, Saskatchewan, August 1983: Seventy-five Native and non-Native women gather to protest Cruise missile testing and the Canadian government's refusal to recognize aboriginal rights to the land it is using for target practice.[2]

Montreal, November 1985: For the third consecutive year, a group of women solemnly interrupt the official Remembrance Day celebration to lay a wreath commemorating the women who were victims of war and read a statement protesting the glorification of war.

WOMEN IN NORTH AMERICA and Western Europe are challenging the military machine and the gender system. There is a link, they say, between the violence and oppressive stereotypes forced upon them and the arms race that threatens to destroy the whole planet. These women reject the patriarchal values which give rise to both problems and attempt to provide "a new vision of liberation and a redefinition of progressive politics" grounded in women's experience.[3]

This vision and these politics have much to offer the peace movement. The analysis of patriarchy put forward by an important segment of the feminist movement[4] provides insights that can deepen our understanding of militarism and serve as the basis for a far-reaching critique of a society in danger of self-destruction. By documenting the extent to which the burden of militarism is borne by women, recent feminist research reveals a broad commonality of interest between the two movements. Feminist group process has been developed, offering ways of working together which seek to empower everyone, rather than a few at the expense of the many.

Patriarchy: From the Nuclear Family to the Nuclear State

The personal is political. This rallying cry of the second wave of feminism from the late-sixties demystifies the arbitrary separation of human experience into two distinct spheres, the public, political world which is identified with men and assigned a high value, and the private, domestic world, accorded only token importance and relegated to women. Strength, reason, and culture are identified with men; instinct and nature with women. On the basis of this dualism, patriarchy socializes men to insensitivity, "scientific objectivity", competition, and women to "feelings", dependence, nurturing.

As Virginia Woolf observed in *Three Guineas*, her pioneering work on militarism and sexism, "The public and the private worlds are inseparably connected; ...the tyrannies and servilities of the one are the tyrannies and servilities of the other."[5] In the personal world of the nuclear family as in the political world of the nuclear state, one law prevails, the law of dominance and submission. Masculinity, reason, and culture are defined not only in opposition to, but also by their ability to dominate femininity, instinct, and nature. Hence the opposition of nature and technology. Hence the male defining himself as male through the subjugation of the "feminine" both within and outside himself. Violence becomes the ultimate expression and sanction of patriarchy.

Making the link between the personal and the political means understanding that our personal relationships are shaped by the power dynamics integral to our society. Thus the exploration of our personal experience is an important means of understanding larger political dynamics. Two major themes that emerge from this exploration by women, and which have been prominent in feminist writings of recent years, are those of violence and nurturing.

Women's experience is deeply marked by the violence of men.

Although this "private" violence long remained hidden, concerted efforts by feminists have brought it to public attention. Its prevalence is such that one writer has described the situation as nothing less than a state of "war against women".[6] The "Centre pour les Victimes d'Assaut Sexuel" in Montreal provides estimates of the number of victims of this war:

- A rape is committed in Canada every 17 minutes.
- One child in ten is a victim of sexual abuse and 90 percent of the victims are girls. In most cases, the abuser belongs to his victim's immediate circle.
- One women in five in Canada will be sexually assaulted at some time in her life, not counting other forms of physical violence.

The omnipresent images of advertising and pornography reinforce the message of women's submission and often provide an incitement to male violence. All women are victims of this violence to the extent that the possibility of violence limits their freedom of movement and keeps them in a state of insecurity and dependence.

Violence against women is compounded by economic exploitation. In Canada, "working women", that is, those belonging to the paid work force, earn less than 60 cents for every dollar earned by men. As well, most of them have a second, non-remunerated, job, that of homemaker, and many are the sole support of one or more children. Their own and their children's financial dependence prevent many women from leaving abusive husbands.

Although the violence against women in our society has been extensively documented, no effective measures have been taken to correct the situation. Still only a tiny proportion of rapes lead to the conviction of the rapist. Services for women who are victims of male violence lack adequate resources and must rely on volunteer labour. Perhaps the most unequivocal expression of the dominant attitude to violence against women came from the 1982 parliamentary committee on domestic violence. Many on the committee, made up of seventeen men and three women, responded with guffaws when informed that one out of ten Canadian wives is beaten by her husband.

The war against women is intricately connected with the militarism of our society; private and public violence reinforce each other in complex ways. Nowhere is the sanction of violence more evident than in the public world. We are constantly surrounded by the symbols of masculine power and institutionalized violence: armed forces patroling land, sea, and air; police forces on the beat at the federal, provincial, and municipal levels; armed security guards protecting private property; and the glamorized versions of these institutions on television and in the movies.

Unlike that in the private world, the violence that occurs in the public world is most often explicitly directed against men. But it is equally marked by misogyny. In fact, misogyny is often used deliberately and systematically as a means of conditioning violent behaviour: for example, in the training of soldiers. Recruits are taught to dehumanize not only the enemy, or any potential enemy, but also women, often through the eroticization of violence.[7] New recruits are continually called "girl" and "faggot" until their behaviour becomes sufficiently aggressive. Only then are they addressed as "men".[8]

The women of the enemy are part of the booty of war, and it is to protect "their" women, so goes the cliché, that men go to war. But who will protect women from their protectors? According to a U.S. government report on domestic violence, "Military service is probably more conducive to violence at home than any other occupation," and even in the civilian population the incidence of wife-beating is higher among veterans than among men who have never served in the armed forces.[9] Growing up the daughter of a military man is poignantly evoked in these lines to her father by Canadian singer-songwriter Marie-Lynn Hammond: "You spend your whole life cocked and ready / Oh Papa can't you see we're not the enemy."[10]

Women also suffer economically because of militarism. Military spending results in the withdrawal of resources and the loss of jobs from those sectors in the economy, such as health services and education, in which women workers are concentrated.[11] Decreased social spending disproportionately affects women because they are poorer and depend more on social programs. Women suffer doubly from the underfunding of programs such as day care for children or nursing homes for the elderly because they often fill the gap as unpaid caregivers.

In patriarchal ideology, war is the quintessential masculine activity. "War is man's work," says Gen. R.H. Barrow of the U.S. Marines. "You've got to protect the manliness of war."[12] Similar opinions were expressed recently by Defence Department officials in Canada seeking an exemption from the new Charter of Rights in order to continue excluding armed forces women from 42 trades and occupations involving combat or near-combat duties.[13]

Yet the services of women are necessary to the military machine in both war and peacetime. Nurses, wives, and prostitutes minister to the troops. Wives, mothers, and sisters "keep the home fires burning", providing incentives for men to fight and a reserve labour force to keep the munitions factories going. As sociologist Cynthia Enloe has shown, the gender system is an essential support to militarism:

> Military forces past and present have not been able to get, keep and reproduce the sorts of soldiers they imagine they need without drawing on

ideological beliefs concerning the different and stratified roles of women and men.... Ignore gender—the social constructions of "femininity" and "masculinity" and the relations between them—and it becomes impossible to adequately explain how military forces have managed to capture and control so much of society's imagination and resources.[14]

The "Better Half": Women's Nurturing and Pacifism

While most of the world's violence is perpetrated by men, most of its nurturing is done by women. Women's association with feelings, nature, and nurturing is not only a measure of our oppression; these subordinate and despised aspects of life have traditionally been a positive resource for women. Possibly they are what has enabled women—and humanity—to survive this long. A real alternative to patriarchy must affirm these values along with the affirmation of women.

Does this mean that women, as child-bearers and nurturers, have a special relationship to life, that they are naturally pacifists? It is unfortunate that women such as Helen Caldicott and Petra Kelly have adopted this notion, which is nothing more than the old oppressive stereotype of women in a deceptively benign form.[15] Besides, if we accept that women are naturally pacifists, we have also to accept that men are naturally violent. Such a view offers very little hope for eliminating militarism.

Rather, we need to acknowledge the potential for creative and destructive energy that exists in all of us, women and men. Masculine competitiveness and violence are socially conditioned just as feminine passivity and dependence are—and equally mutable. The antidote to militarism is indeed a good dose of the values traditionally associated with women. But it must be accompanied by the determination that these become *human* values, cultivated by all, and not just in half, of humanity. Adrienne Rich writes:

> The mother's battle for her child—with sickness, with poverty, with war, with all the forces of exploitation and callousness that cheapen human life—needs to become a common human battle, waged in love and in the passion for survival.[16]

Feminism and the Peace Movement

The peace movement, in Canada as in other Western countries, is broad and diverse, and encompasses many points of view. One might expect it to be receptive to feminism. But the peace movement is as much marked by patriarchal values as any institution of our society. Both in theory and practice, it largely ignores the oppression of women, and tends to reproduce the same power relations found in the society at large. The tendency to favour limited unified objectives (such as stopping Cruise testing or Star Wars), centralized control, and speaking with one voice restricts the possibility for radical analysis and egalitarian practice.

Although women make up the majority of the movement's rank and file, its acknowledged leaders and experts are predominantly male. If there are any doubts on this score, a cursory look at the list of speakers at almost any conference, or of writers for peace movement publications (including this book) should dispel them. Even at the workshop on "Women and Peace" at a 1985 conference in Montreal, two out of three speakers were male, but perhaps this should be taken as an indication of the enormous importance accorded to this subject by the conference organizers.[17]

Given women's under-representation in the leadership of the peace movement, it is not surprising that their specific concerns are not reflected in the movement's priorities. A male activist who made a comprehensive review of major peace movement books and periodicals published in Canada reports that "analyses and discourse of the movement" hardly refer "to the link between patriarchy and militarism, between masculinity and the arms race, between private life and public life, and between the war against women and war in general".[18] In the peace movement, as elsewhere in public life, women's concerns are subjected to a double process of invalidation, which has been described by political scientist Jean Elshtain:

> Concerns that arise "naturally" from [women's] position in the private sphere...are deemed private expressions of personal values, but any hard-nosed realistic talk about power from women means that they have forfeited the right to represent to the public sphere the private world that they have presumably forsaken.[19]

It is worth remembering that in Canada as in the United States, one of the main roots of the second wave of feminism was in the new left anti-war movement of the 1960s. That movement's vision of a liberatory politics, combined with its failure to confront the issue of men's power over women, sparked the emergence of a separate women's liberation movement.[20]

Today's peace movement is being challenged by feminists strengthened by the experience of the women's movement over the past 15 years. These peace activists, refusing to be silenced by the fear of "dividing the movement", are insisting that women's concerns, far from being secondary to the "real questions", are fundamental to the issues of war and peace. Only the exclusion of these concerns divides the movement. Through actions such as those at Greenham, Comiso, and Cole Bay, women are telling the peace movement that it is not enough to oppose this weapon or that weapon but that we need to strike at the roots of militarism by opposing the patriarchal values and institutions that sustain it. They are reaching across the man-made boundaries of nations and blocs to make their message heard. Witness to this is the open letter signed by women in five European countries, East and West, where there has been deployment of new U.S. and Soviet nuclear weapons.*

The peace movement is being challenged to confront sexism in practice as well as theory. At the level of larger groups, feminists' demands have been relatively modest, for example, that child care be provided during conferences (it rarely is, in my experience) or that half of the delegates to a convention be women (a demand refused by the Liaison Committee of the European Nuclear Disarmament [END] Convention, July 1985, in Amsterdam).[21]

It is at the grassroots level of the peace movement that feminists have tended to be most active, at least in part because feminist process is most applicable in smaller groups. Concern with process is characteristic of feminism, for if the personal is political, then our interpersonal relations must necessarily reflect our political ideals. The following elements have emerged from intensive experimentation with group process based on feminist principles:

- organizing in small groups, so that each individual can have the most input possible;
- building non-hierarchical structures, so that both leadership and support functions may be shared by all members of the group;
- sharing information, skills, and support;
- consensual decision-making;
- paying attention to the emotional climate in a group;
- making the connection between people's experience and "the larger questions";
- using means consistent with the ends sought;
- acknowledging and dealing with sexist, racist, or other oppressive dynamics when they occur.[22]

These are guidelines, not rules. Perhaps the most visible effect of their application in the peace movement would be a more equitable sharing of responsibility between men and women. But they go much further than that to provide for a group process that encourages everyone to contribute fully, that disempowers no one, and that allows each individual to relate

---

* See previous chapter, box headed "For Detente from below...An open letter by women from East and West..."

personal experience to the movement's aims and, in turn, to other major social issues.

The age-old dream to put an end to war is a long-term project. We have not only to reverse the proliferation of weapons that threatens life on the planet, we must also confront a society that is prepared to use these weapons in defence of its values. We need a peace movement that commands people's commitment over the long haul by speaking to their experience and concerns and by offering a vision of society that is a real alternative to militarism. Feminist analysis and practice can contribute to this process.

Notes

1. "Notes," *END: Journal of European Nuclear Disarmament*, April/May 1983, p. 4.

2. Vye Bouvier, "Women's Peace Camp—On the Border," *New Breed Journal*, October 1983, p. 18.

3. Angela Miles, *Feminist Radicalism in the 1980s* (Montreal, 1985), p. 30.

4. I am here referring to that tendency in feminism, often described as "integrative feminism", which seeks "the end of male dualism and the establishment of a community whose basic organizing principles are connection and co-operation rather than separation and opposition". Miles, *Feminist Radicalism*, p. 23.

5. Virginia Woolf, *Three Guineas* (London, 1938), p. 258.

6. Barbara Roberts, "No Safe Place: The War Against Women," in *Our Generation*, Vol. 15, No. 4, Spring 1983.

7. Examples abound in Warnock, "Patriarchy is a Killer: What People Concerned About Peace and Justice Should Know", *Reweaving the Web of Life: Feminism and Nonviolence*, ed. Pam McAllister (Philadelphia, 1982), p. 22.

8. Helen Michalowski, "The Army Will Make a 'Man' Out of You", in McAllister, *Reweaving the Web*, p. 330.

9. Quoted in Cynthia Enloe, *Does Khaki Become You?: The Militarization of Women's Lives* (Boston, 1983), p. 87.

10. Quoted in Heather Menzies, " 'Our time is now'—the Canadian Women's Music and Cultural Festival," *Canadian Woman Studies/ Les Cahiers de la Femme*, Vol. 6, No. 2, Spring 1985, p. 90.

11. Marion Anderson, *Neither Jobs Nor Security: Women's Unemployment and the Pentagon Budget* (Lansing, Michigan: Employment Research Associates).

12. Quoted in Enloe, *Does Khaki Become You?*, pp. 153-154.

13. *The Gazette*, Montreal, 20 July 1985, p. A-9.

14. Enloe, *Does Khaki Become You?*, p. 212.

15. Helen Caldicott, *Missile Envy* (New York, 1984); and Petra Kelly, *Fighting for Hope* (Boston, 1984), p. 104.

16. *Of Woman Born: Motherhood as Experience and Institution* (New York, 1977), p. 285.

17. The conference referred to is that of the Future Studies Association at the Learned Societies Conferences, June 1985, at the Université de Montréal.

18. Alan Silverman, "Feminism and the Canadian Peace Movement: Some Reflections of a Male Activist," unpublished paper, December 1984, p. 56.

19. Jean Bethke Elshtain, "On Beautiful Souls, Just Warriors and Feminist Consciousness," *Women's Studies Int. Forum*, Vol. 5, No. 3/4, 1982, p. 347.

20. Miles, *Feminist Radicalism*, p. 4 and p. 32, note 5.

21. Fiona Weir, "Women and END Convention", *Disarmament Campaigns*, April 1985, p. 14.

22. Cf. Leslie Cagan, "Feminism and Militarism," in *Beyond Survival: New Directions for the Disarmament Movement*, ed. Michael Albert and David Dellinger (Boston, 1983), p. 106.

Community Disarmament Initiatives

Andrea Levy

> Our tiny residential community...is under no illusion that this action will bring the arms race to a halt. On the other hand, we refuse to be paralyzed by the enormity of the problem. If our little piece of the world is joined by enough other pieces, maybe we can 'peace it all together' before it's too late.[1]　　　　　　　　　　　　—Grandmont Community Association

IN DECEMBER 1984 the local authority in Grandmont, Michigan, declared the area a nuclear free zone. Their statement summarizes the intent and hopes of thousands of communities across the globe which have, in one manner or another, begun resisting collaboration in national government policies of nuclear weapons proliferation.

The forms that this refusal takes vary from community to community but the declaration of nuclear free zones is a common denominator. All testify to a burgeoning international grassroots peace movement which has grown sceptical of the claims of national government to support arms reduction and doubtful of the efficacy of high level political negotiations. This movement is strongest in Western Europe (Britain, Wales, Ireland, West Germany, Italy, Spain, Holland, and Norway, for example) but also has deep roots in Australia, Japan, Canada, the United States and, especially, New Zealand.[2]

President Dwight Eisenhower once remarked that, "People want peace so much that one of these days governments had better get out of the way and let them have it." Regrettably, few governments have followed his advice. Indeed, the main stimulant of local disarmament initiatives and especially the nuclear free zone movement has been the lack of responsiveness of national government to popular protest against the escalation of the arms race and its concomitant threat of global annihilation, as well as its immediate consequences in the form of ecological damage, grossly inflated military budgets and the drain on national resources. Often, concern with the arms race is accompanied by a growing awareness of its implications for national issues such as poverty, unemployment, and the environment. Faced with the apparent intransigence of the central state, communities began consciously seeking nonviolent ways of challenging defence policies and priorities. In small towns and large cities people began to assume responsibilities that their governments appeared unwilling to assume and to use their local authorities as a vehicle of change. The spirit and strategy informing these developments are neatly summed up in the slogan of the West German Green Party: "Think globally, act locally."

The concept of the nuclear free zone (NFZ) or nuclear weapons free zone offered a powerful symbol, easily adapted to local conditions, around which a community could rally. The concept itself originated in the 1950s and gained currency with the signing of a number of international NFZ treaties such as that concerning the Antarctic in 1959, and those concerning outer space and Latin America in 1967. As well, several countries, including Japan and Austria, have had NFZ clauses written into their constitutions or adopted as national policy. The NFZ concept was appropriated by local movements in the 1970s and the idea of individual communities declaring themselves NFZs spread quickly and traversed national borders in a relatively short time.

An NFZ declaration can involve a general statement against the nuclear arms race or it can have specific content, calling for or introducing a ban on research, production, testing, transportation, storage, and deployment of nuclear weapons, their components, and their delivery systems. The latter type can vary to include the siting of nuclear reactors and the disposal of nuclear waste. Or it can be more restricted in scope, dealing, for instance, exclusively with deployment. These declarations can be purely symbolic, formulated as demands or resolutions, or legally-binding, formulated, for instance, as ordinances. They have been achieved by petitioning local governments, holding special referenda, and placing proposed measures on local election ballots. Whatever the particular features, the basic idea is universal: When a community declares itself a NFZ it is saying it wants no part of the nuclear arms race.

There are currently close to 3,000 NFZs in 18 countries around the world. In 1958, the world's first local NFZ was declared in Handa, Japan, in protest against atmospheric nuclear weapons tests being conducted in the Pacific. It is hardly surprising after the experience of Hiroshima and Nagasaki that a great part of the Japanese population is devoted to the goal of nuclear disarmament. However, Japan's NFZ movement has only gained momentum since the late 1970s as a result of a new push for remilitarization. In spite of the renunciation of war article set out in the Japanese Constitution (imposed by the United States after Japan's military defeat in 1945) and the three non-nuclear principles—"Japan will not produce, possess or let others bring in nuclear weapons"—adopted as national policy in 1968, in the 1980s Japan has been under considerable pressure from the United States and the Japanese right wing to build up its "defence capabilities" over and above providing the U.S. with military bases and other forms of integration into NATO nuclear strategy. The current government seems inclined to bend to this pressure.

In 1975 Fitzroy, Australia, became the first town in which a local authority declared the area a NFZ. The administration acted in support of the Australian Movement Against Uranium Mining, which called on town councils to ban all non-medical nuclear materials. Since then, 96 NFZs have been declared and the movement has been bringing pressure to bear upon the Australian government, which has failed to make good on the NFZ plank in its election platform.

In Britain, the development of a NFZ movement was linked to refusal of central government civil defence programs and the related duties imposed on local councils. It gave rise to a wide range of activities initiated, funded, or promoted by local authorities, the most impressive of which are the disarmament efforts of the Greater London Council, a regional authority with jurisdiction over a number of London boroughs. The GLC has since been dismantled by the Conservative government.

In the United States, the NFZ trend grew largely out of frustration with apparent government disregard of the nuclear freeze campaign and the perceived lack of political will to realize significant arms control agreements. The movement has gained momentum since 1980 with the renewal of Cold War ideology and the Reagan administration's espousal of the concept of limited nuclear war, of first strike capability, and of the Strategic Defense Initiative or Star Wars.

Beyond the primary motives of pressuring or bypassing governments caught up in the illogic of the arms race, local disarmament campaigns are attractive to organizers and resident populations for a number of particular reasons. For one, they are able to make the arms race concrete in the public consciousness by demonstrating that it is not something taking place exclusively in Washington and Moscow. The point local campaigns drive home is that activities related to nuclear weapons are going on where people live and work. Local industries may have defence contracts to manufacture nuclear weapons components; the weapons themselves may be stored or deployed in a community's backyard; nuclear materials destined for the arms industry may be transported over back roads or city streets; a port may be harbouring ships carrying nuclear weapons, and so on. Even where no such activities are taking place, communities are implicated in the arms race if only indirectly through the purchase of products manufactured by, or the award of city contracts to, companies with major defence contracts. Information on these activities makes the issue of the arms race less abstract, easier to grasp and confront, and often provides a perceptible target upon which protest energies can be focused.

By way of example, in Woensdrecht, Holland, local opposition to the arms race galvanized around the Dutch government's decision to deploy Cruise missiles in the town in June 1983. As a result of popular pressure, the city council resolved to obstruct deployment. In spite of resistance from the mayor and aldermen, the city became a plaintiff in a lawsuit against the state that sought to prevent the Dutch government from deploying the Cruise. Since then an astonishing 20,000 individual cities and institutions in the Netherlands have undertaken similar litigation.[3]

Admittedly, having a missile sited in one's village is an extreme case of the arms race rendered tangible. However, deployment is only one of numerous activities that give rise to organized local protest. In Oak Ridge, Tennessee, home of the factory complex of weapons contractor Martin Marietta, a network of weapons shipment trackers has grown up composed largely of volunteers from the Catholic, Quaker, and Mennonite religious communities. The goal of this group is to identify trucks carrying nuclear weapons on their way for repair or replacement. When a courier is spotted, the community network moves into action, staging roadside protests and notifying similar networks in the states through which the shipments are likely to pass. Because of the intentional secrecy surrounding these shipments, the federal government and the drivers take pains to avoid identification, going so far as to send out decoy trucks to distract protestors from the genuine article.[4] Within these religious communities across the U.S., projects have also been undertaken to divest institutional funds from nuclear industries, to reject designation of their buildings as fallout shelters and to convert existing fallout shelters into soup kitchens and community centres, thus making a simple and direct link between spiralling defence spending and the drastic reduction of social services.

The nuclear free zone campaign can address all the issues—deployment, transportation, etc.—at the local level. To select just one of many examples, in the San Juan islands of Washington, a successful NFZ campaign was waged by a group called Islanders for Nuclear Arms Control. It circulated petitions, held workshops and public meetings, placed advertisements in local papers, wrote letters to the editor, displayed material in a public library about nuclear weapons, and set up information booths. The campaign gained a great deal of support, including that of the county sheriff who told organizers that if the ordinances were to prohibit the transportation of nuclear weapons through county waters he would, in the event of a violation, happily notify the Trident Submarine commander.[5]

The Importance of Victories

Local disarmament campaigns clearly provide a major opportunity for public outreach and education. They help individuals to realize that as long as they do not take an active stand against the arms race, they are, in some sense, a party to it. Further, they help communities to begin perceiving themselves as small links in a vast chain and to recognize that every weakened or broken link contributes to the severance of that chain.

Moreover, these types of actions contribute to a sense of empowerment on the part of participants and organizers. As a result of directly working in their own communities towards an immediate goal, participants learn that, in contrast with simply petitioning other levels of government, they must rely on themselves to begin the disarmament process. They have an essential role to play. The local campaigns provide an opportunity to take a step towards achieving a measure of local self determination. As Don Skinner suggests, "Communities must assert their rights to control their living space and then join with each other to form the foundations of a viably self reliant bio-region. By establishing a free zone, a symbolic and practical blow is struck at nuclear culture, and community self control is advanced."[6]

Furthermore, where local authorities are used as a channel the results are frequently positive because city councils are more likely to respond to popular pressure. There is at least one case, in Nerima, Japan, where a local government's refusal to adopt a nuclear free zone resolution was a major factor in its subsequent election defeat. The new council adopted the resolution by unanimous vote.[7]

In their article "Organizing for a Nuclear Free Cambridge", Rick Schreuer and Eric Segal identify this as the fundamental appeal of NFZ campaigns: "Eminently more winnable than the large national campaigns that can give rise to such despair, NFZ organizing can produce a tangible, significant victory in a finite period of time."[8] Local campaigns, particularly of the NFZ variety, are engaging because, while they are organized independently on a community basis and do not rely on directives "from above", they are not isolated initiatives.

There is a growing awareness that community resistance to the arms race is manifesting itself nationally and internationally and that each individual campaign is a part of a decentralized but connected global movement. This sense of connection and solidarity can lead to some interesting developments on a regional level. In England, for example, a national conference of NFZ authorities was held in 1981 (by this time 119 English NFZs were in existence) and a national steering committee was appointed. The committee was assigned a co-ordinating-advisory function and also undertook the preparation of reports on civil defence, peace education, public safety, and other NFZ related matters. Similarly, in Japan the National Association of Nuclear Free Local Authorities was formed in 1984 to promote co-operation. In the United States, Nuclear Free America acts as a resource centre and clearing house allowing for NFZ networking. At the level of administrators, Local Elected Officials for Social Responsibility provides a forum of exchange and co-operation.

There is also information exchange and discussion on the international level. Two international conferences of NFZ local authorities have been held, the first in Manchester, England, in April 1984 and the second in Cordoba, Spain, in March 1985. In many countries, regional NFZ initiatives are being launched, inspired by the local campaigns and as a result of collaborative local efforts. In the United States, for example, statewide NFZ campaigns are underway in various states, including Alaska, California, Massachusetts, and Oregon. Both in themselves and through the international exchange and co-operation they generate, local campaigns provide an essential complement to projects of more ambitious scope such as the Campaign for Nuclear Disarmament (CND) intra-Europe NFZ proposal, the Nuclear Free Pacific Movement, and the Balkan NFZ initiative to which the Papandreou government in Greece is committed.

From Symbolism to the Force of Law

The local NFZ was first conceived mainly as a symbolic gesture and an expression of public will. But in the past few years there has been a trend among local campaigns towards comprehensive resolutions and the inclusion of legally-binding provisions, nuclear free contracting and investment policies, and penalties for violations of the ordinances. In West Germany, for example, the NFZ campaigns have given way to ABC Free campaigns (atomic, biological, and chemical weapons free zones) and to struggles involving issues of federal versus local powers. Opponents of council ordinances in the FRG argued (as they do everywhere) that defence is a federal government domain and therefore NFZ or ABC Free declarations were outside municipal jurisdiction. Predictably, the Ministry of Internal Affairs concurred and prohibited councils from dealing with nuclear weapons storage or transport. The courts, on the other hand, were less unanimous in their judgements. In May 1984, the administrative court of the state of Baden-Wurttemburg concluded that nuclear weapons are a threat to public security and awarded local communities the right to consider legislation regarding the deployment of U.S. weapons. As a result of that decision, the Ministry of Internal Affairs repealed its restrictive order.[9]

In Vancouver, the city amended the zoning, development, and fire by-laws in order to effectively prohibit the storage and transportation of nuclear weapons and their components in the territory of the city. When a private citizen legally challenged the right of a municipality to hold a NFZ referendum, the British Columbia Supreme Court ruled that such an action was within municipal jurisdiction because of its relation to public health and welfare.

The idea of using the award of city contracts as a tool in local disarmament efforts is gaining popularity. In England in 1982, the Southwark Borough Council decided to remove those companies involved in building missile silos at Greenham Common from their approved list of contractors. Similarly in Holland, many NFZs are refusing to do business with construction companies working on Cruise missile bases. In the United States in 1983, the city of Takoma Park, Maryland, was the first to pass a legally-binding NFZ ordinance including clauses concerning nuclear free contracting and investment policies (see box). This city had the good fortune to have been nuclear free in the first place. Still, the objective of the "Takoma Park Nuclear Free Zone Act" was to maintain that status and to adopt some practical measures regarding the use of city funds.

These measures were not without effect. In keeping with the portion of the Act that states, "The City of Takoma Park shall grant no awards or contracts for any purpose to any person, firm, corporation or entity which is knowingly or intentionally engaged in the development, research, testing, evaluation, production, maintenance, storage, transportation and/or disposal of nuclear weapons or their components," the city rejected bids for police radios from General Electric and Motorola, both producers of nuclear weapons components. The city found an alternative supplier and ended by saving money on the final purchase.[10]

Similarly, in Amherst, Massachusetts, an ordinance similar to Takoma's forced town officials to cancel a contract for word processors purchased from Harris Corp., a Defence Department contractor.

Opposition to these types of initiatives tends to be well organized and concerted. NFZ campaigns in Santa Cruz, California, and Cambridge, Massachusetts, for example, have sparked resistance from major defence companies. In Santa Cruz, Lockheed spent $300,000 on an anti-NFZ campaign—as opposed to $31,000 raised by campaign supporters—and threatened to close its plant, which provided an annual payroll of $11 million. The NFZ initiative brought an unusually large voter turnout and while it won the polls in the city of Santa Cruz, it was defeated county-wide, 63 per cent against, 37 per cent in favour.

In Cambridge, where many local businesses had nuclear weapons related contracts, a group of prestigious individuals in the community helped to launch an expensive anti-NFZ campaign. This contributed to the reversal of precampaign polls that showed a majority in favour of the NFZ. There, the weapons industries spent a record $550,000. The NFZ measure failed by an 18 per cent margin in spite of efforts on the part of NFZ supporters to demonstrate the long-term negative economic impact of military industry.

With the Cambridge experience in mind, the drafters of the state-wide NFZ initiative in Massachusetts addressed the economic issues in the actual wording of the measure. In addition to outlawing the development and production of nuclear weapons, the state would provide incentives for affected industries to convert to non-defence work and would provide benefits to workers laid off as a consequence of the NFZ Act.

The concept of military-industrial conversion has a fundamental role to play in the discussion of disarmament and must be raised, explained, and included as policy, particularly when defence related jobs are at issue. Increasingly, local disarmament campaigns are making the point that military industry is harmful to the economy, that it is a poor generator of employment, that it reduces the competitive strength of civilian industry on the world market, and that it drains valuable human, financial, material, and natural resources. Military spending does not, contrary to the stubborn myth, contribute to the economic well-being of a nation.

Still, local NFZ campaigns are less likely to be successful on the home territory of the weapons contractors. Yet the fact that the industry feels genuinely threatened by them is indicative of the importance of even an unsuccessful campaign. And contrary to what one might imagine, defeat does not necessarily result in demobilization. The educational process integral to the campaign can galvanize a formerly inactive opposition.

In spite of the defeats in Santa Cruz and Cambridge, U.S. NFZ campaigns continue to be waged close to the heart of the nuclear weapons industry. Organizers in Berkeley and Alameda County in California planned to put an extremely comprehensive NFZ measure on the November 1986 ballot. The David and Goliath quality of this particular case stems from the fact that the areas in question are home both to Lawrence Livermore Laboratory, which does the bulk of American nuclear weapons research, and to Alameda naval air station, where it is suspected nuclear weapons are stored.

Courtroom Battles

The type of NFZ initiative that attempts to inscribe provisions in local law is also the subject of considerable legal controversy and some litigation in the United States, especially when the stakes are high. A recent struggle in New York City provides a good illustration.

The city adopted a symbolic NFZ resolution in 1984, and test of the resolution was forthcoming. The federal government had chosen Stapleton, Staten Island, as a Navy homeport. A sum of $280 million had been earmarked for construction of the base for seven U.S. warships, some of which would likely carry nuclear weapons. Consequently, a coalition of antinuclear groups began collecting signatures in order to force the city to hold a referendum on the homeport issue. Over a hundred thousand signatures were collected. A favourable vote in the referendum—and polls predicted public support—would have prohibited the city from selling or leasing property and from appropriating or expending funds for the purpose of a military facility. It would have prevented the city from granting any franchise, permit, license, use, or consent to use of any city owned property or street in conjunction with the Staten Island base.

New York Mayor Koch, along with a number of senators, brought suit against the proposed referendum, arguing that the Navy base would be an economic boon for the port and that the city has an obligation to do its part for national defence. A State Supreme Court Justice who ruled on the case concluded that the referendum was unconstitutional and ordered it off the November 1985 election ballot. Justice Kuffner said the referendum conflicted with the authority granted to Congress to provide for the common defence of the nation. He stated, "If a state or local law exists which might upset that delicate balance existing between the federal and state sovereignties, the state or local law must give way."[11] He also revealed his personal opinions by quoting another court justice to the effect that, "It is important also to consider, that the surest means of avoiding war is to be prepared for it in peace."[12]

In striking contrast, lawyers in Santa Cruz, California, argued, "To give the federal government absolutely unfettered power to regulate its citizens in the name of defence or 'war powers' is to upset the delicate balance between federal interests and traditional states' rights reserved to local control."[13] Further, they argued, "The nuclear weapons [free zone] initiative is one of the few legal and practical means available for people... to claim that the limited constitutional mandate for national defence is being abused by manufacturing and testing of first strike and massively destructive nuclear weapons systems."[14]

NFZ defence lawyers use a host of arguments in their efforts to defend the constitutionality of the measures. They also invoke international law—the International Laws of War (1907), the Nuremberg Principles (1945), and the Geneva Convention (1945)—which suggests that nuclear weapons are illegal and that municipalities are upholding international law in face of national government violations.

The legal controversy in the United States is a complex one and, for all practical purposes, only the Supreme Court will resolve it in any definitive manner. While no NFZ case had come before it by the mid-1980s, one interesting precedent bodes well for the movement. In 1983 the Supreme Court ruled that state and local governments are not pre-empted by the federal government in controlling and regulating nuclear industry. The Court decided to uphold a California moratorium on the construction of nuclear power plants in spite of the Atomic Energy Act which, according to numerous legal opinions, prohibits states from imposing conditions on the construction of nuclear power plants.

In any event, even if the courts were to systematically interpret the law as excluding the NFZs, this would provide a clear demonstration of a fundamental contradiction between unlimited federal powers of national defence and the powers concerning the protection of the health and welfare of citizens traditionally reserved to local authorities. A similar but more dramatic effect would be produced were the courts to rule in favour of the NFZs and were Congress to pass specific legislation pre-empting local laws.

Although the examples above are drawn from the United States, similar legal issues and implications for the powers of the state exist wherever there are NFZs. (The same issues also apply where there are no legal NFZs, as in Denmark where eight NFZs have been declared even though parliament has twice rejected the right of towns to create NFZs.) Any final victory for the peace movement at the local level can only come about through a mass movement prepared to support significant political, social, and economic changes. But legal victories, such as the one in Baden-Wurttemburg, can afford a "bourgeois legitimacy" to the cause, thereby making it more difficult for opponents to challenge its constitutionality. They can also help broaden the disarmament constituency, especially within the middle class. Such victories alter the relations of power slightly in favour of the disarmament forces.

Education and Local Initiative

Opposition to NFZ campaigns, especially in their initial stages, does not issue solely from central states, nuclear weapons industries, and courts. Reservations are often expressed within resident populations. NFZ campaigns are frequently criticized as sincere but misguided because they point in the direction of unilateral disarmament. (No one actually comes out and says they are opposed to peace.) Echoes of this argument are periodically encountered in the general population. Organizers can more easily respond to this charge if they espouse a clear position of non-alignment attributing responsibility for the arms race to both the superpowers. Perhaps the strongest argument is that trust building has to start somewhere, and that NFZs are intended to start such a process. In a letter to the Ashland, Oregon, City Council in support of a NFZ resolution, a member of Citizen Action for Lasting Security argued:

> The suggestion has been made that the Nuclear Free Zone law, if adopted by local jurisdictions throughout the United States would be tantamount to unilateral disarmament. This is an interesting but certainly remote hypothetical scenario. The Nuclear Free Zone concept involves a step by step trust building exercise that stands in stark contrast to the hostile war posturing of today's international scene. It does not deny the existence of conflict or expect conflict to cease. It does say that nuclear war is not one of the choices for solving conflicts. It is a statement of morality and conscience. It is a bilateral scheme wherein denuclearized zones are established as a basis for negotiating verifiable nuclear free zone agreements with cities and countries in Eastern Block nations. The concept may catch the imagination of more and more cities, states and countries until we have reduced the number of nuclearized zones to just two, Moscow and Washington, D.C. Perhaps then they will get the message.[15]

The "what about the Russians?" response to local disarmament efforts has served to open up discussion on a variety of issues and provides an opportunity to address the myths of Cold War ideology. The paramount point is that nuclear weapons do not offer security in any way, shape, or form. It is also essential to discuss issues such as the difference between offensive and defensive non-nuclear weapons, the independent peace movements in Eastern Europe, and especially the idea that the Soviet government does not express the views of Soviet citizens on the question of disarmament any more than the U.S. government represents its citizens.

One innovative way that communities have found to counter the Cold War climate and to address concerns in a direct fashion is "twinning", which involves adopting a sister city in the Soviet Union or Eastern Europe and promoting human contact and cultural exchange. This type of action fits nicely with the entire strategy of "detente from below"—the idea that ordinary citizens can overcome the hostile blocs mentality and engage in constructive dialogue. By way of example, the citizens in Eureka, Montana, wrote a letter to Rebrikha in Central Siberia. Eureka had the help of a business professor at Portland State University who matched U.S. and Soviet cities of similar size and geographic characteristics. With their letter, the Eurekans enclosed a local newspaper and a picture postcard. In return they received a seven-page letter signed by 33 residents of Rebrikha, a copy of *Pravda*, and a photograph of the local department store. Exchanges such as these can go a long way towards destroying the Cold War myth of the Other as unapproachably alien.

While in most instances the initiative to engage an individual local authority in disarmament actions comes from groups within the resident population, many mayors and local councils have been co-operative and enthusiastic. As Mayor Motoshima of Nagasaki remarked during the 1985 First World Conference of Mayors for Peace Through Inter-City Solidarity:

> We think that efforts for disarmament, especially for the abolition of nuclear weapons, and moves towards establishing everlasting world peace should not be expected only of the central governments of countries. Since the victims of war, especially nuclear war, are the cities and citizens living therein, it is indispensable for urban administrations, as well as individuals, to share the responsibility for creating peace.[16]

There are few urban administrations that have taken that burden of responsibility more seriously than did the Greater London Council. The GLC declared London a NFZ in 1982 and subsequently organized a wide range of peace activities along with a major media and public relations campaign. It used Council funds both to support peace groups and to undertake special projects of its own. In 1984 it established the Nuclear Policy Unit to undertake new policy development work on nuclear issues. It has published and made widely available a series of attractive and readable documents dealing with issues such as the medical consequences of nuclear war, the significance of nuclear free zones, the negative impact of defence spending on the London economy, and the myth of civil defence.

On the last topic the GLC is particularly incisive. Its pamphlet "Blackout to Whitewash" documents the history of British civil defence policy and practice from the First World War, while "London and Civil Defence" illustrates, among other things, how government funds are wasted on civil defence planning for war when no money is available for emergency planning in the event of major accidents or natural disaster. These pamphlets are concise, to the point, and marked with humour: "A wide range of staff will have civil defence duties, according to the Home Office. The Home Office seems to be expecting staff to be able to turn up for work after a nuclear attack, despite blast, fire, radiation and the effects of nuclear winter."[17]

Perhaps most significantly, in 1983 the GLC established an independent regional conversion council for London. The council's mandate was to "research the conversion of military production in London to civilian use, and to give practical assistance to companies and workers in the defence industry in establishing 'alternative-use committees' and in identifying non-military products". This conversion council included representatives from the defence industry, local London boroughs, the Campaign for Nuclear Disarmament, Scientists Against Nuclear Arms, and the GLC itself.

Vancouver provides another example of ongoing co-operation and innovation at the level of a local administration. In 1985, after several years of disarmament related resolutions and collaboration with local peace groups, the City Council created a special committee on peace to pursue its disarmament efforts and to encourage other Canadian municipalities to undertake projects of their own and to join forces with Vancouver in concerted actions.

Even where independent council initiatives and budgetary support for local peace groups are not forthcoming, in most instances there is at least one local elected official who can be counted upon for active support of local disarmament efforts. However, it is not unusual to encounter a majority of council members who are either hostile to the peace movement to begin with or quickly influenced by external pressures. For example, the Drapeau administration in Montreal (where a large part of Canada's military industry is located) was always unwilling so much as to discuss any disarmament-related questions. In Kauai County, Hawaii, the council approved a NFZ ordinance on first reading and then unanimously defeated it as a result of pressure from the Navy and after a public hearing during which the director of the Chamber of Commerce told the council it had better reconsider its approval.

As a member of the Michigan Alliance for Disarmament remarked in reference to the defeated Ann Arbor NFZ initiative, "It is a grave error to assume that City Hall is on our side. Especially in areas where there is much money involved in the nuclear weapons and nuclear war industry, local government is not likely to look favourably on people who are making...trouble for business."[18]

Limits and Potential of the NFZ Movement

In theory, the proliferation of NFZs, along with other kinds of community disarmament initiatives, challenges the traditional powers of the central state to pursue "national defence" in its usual unfettered fashion. In practice, however, there are limits to what local movements are able to do. Even when backed by a strong popular mandate, local authorities tend to succumb to pressure from the central state and the industries that profit from the arms race. This pressure can, for example, take the form of tacit or explicit threats regarding job loss or future allocation of funds. There is also the possibility of legislation that prevents the creation of local NFZs. But such heavy-handed action is generally a last resort given the reluctance of the central state to come into open confrontation with local authorities backed by strong public support.

Popular support for disarmament efforts can also be diffused by raising the spectre of economic hardship as a result of possible defence industry relocation. As this type of appeal touches a more concrete and immediate public preoccupation, it is vital that disarmament campaigns be accompanied by education about the deleterious economic effects of the arms race and the advantages of industrial conversion. However, the Cambridge and Santa Cruz examples testify to the difficulty of such efforts faced with the unlimited resources of the defence contractors.

Implicitly and explicitly the local movements are challenging the all-embracing powers of central states, particularly in matters of national security. But so long as nation states continue to exist in their present form and in symbiotic relationship with military industrial complexes, it seems that the short-term practical effects of combined local disarmament initiatives are quite restricted.

Nonetheless their value should not be underestimated. The consequences of determined popular non-compliance, especially through the channels of local government, are multifold and far-reaching. Firstly, it can in certain circumstances lead to unyielding positions in favour of disarmament on the part of national governments.

New Zealand is a singular example in this respect, especially in contrast with Australia. Both countries elected Labour governments with NFZ platforms. In New Zealand, Prime Minister David Lange upheld his party's pledge by refusing permission to a U.S. Navy destroyer to visit New Zealand's port as part of annual ANZUS Treaty exercises because, as is its policy, the United States refused to confirm or deny the presence of nuclear weapons on the ship. It would have been impossible for him to risk the already evident consequences of such a decision in the form of U.S. retaliation without the existing massive support at the grassroots, community level. More than half the population of the country live in local NFZs.

In Australia on the other hand, Prime Minister Robert Hawke gave in to U.S. pressure and even declared himself willing to discuss sanctions against New Zealand with the United States. However, grassroots pressure, along with severe reaction from his own party, did manage to force Hawke to cancel a secret defence agreement with the United States involving testing of the MX missile.

Secondly, serious community efforts have led to numerous small but significant victories at the local level itself, which at least serve to frustrate the policies and practices of government and defence industry. In Kobe, Japan, a NFZ and a leading world port, the dockworkers union initiated a struggle that forced the U.S. Navy to abandon its base there in 1974. Since that time, the city has steadfastly refused to allow the entry of military ships from any country that refuses to confirm the absence of nuclear weapons. Kobe is the only nuclear free port in Japan. In England, 20 NFZ councils refused to participate in the 1982 civil defence exercise "Hard Rock" and the government was forced to cancel the operation. (In response, the government introduced new Civil Defence Regulations but the councils are finding ways to frustrate their implementation.)

In Santa Cruz, California, in spite of the defeat of the local NFZ initiative, local authorities refused Lockheed a grading permit to expand its facilities to accommodate production of parts for the Trident II missile. Massive pressure had been put on the Planning Commission from a broad coalition of local groups that mobilized public support. These groups used the formal argument that the Lockheed expansion would entail the destruction of 113 trees whereas the original permit required their protection. Local citizens testified at the Planning Commission hearing on the matter, as did Lockheed itself. And while two of the three commissioners who voted against the permit used the trees to justify their decisions, it was the most conservative member of the commission who broke the 2-2 tie by openly declaring that he opposed the permit because he wanted to impede the manufacture of the Trident. Lockheed appealed the decision to the County Board of Supervisors but lost in another 3-2 vote.

Both Lockheed and the citizens of Santa Cruz were aware that production of the Trident II would not be blocked as a result of the prevented expansion. But, as activists noted, "This is a nation in which the wheels of government have never yet paused on the road to nuclear annihilation. The denial of this grading permit...in Santa Cruz is a small but important brake on the arms race. And we need all the brakes we can get."[19]

Finally, the process of education and mobilization fundamental to community disarmament initiatives ensures contact and dialogue with many uninformed or inactive people. Grassroots peace work reaches people who have never seriously considered the nuclear weapons issue before. It speaks to those who live with the psychological distortion induced by the fear of nuclear war, but who perceive themselves as powerless. This is especially true of young people who wonder about the point of making plans when their future appears so uncertain. It also offers a chance to present and make relevant to their daily lives the "other side" to people who have been exposed to only one set of arguments. It provides sympathetic but undecided people with the intellectual ammunition needed to defeat in their own minds the twisted logic of the arms race. It dispels myths and builds transnational bridges.

Developing a strong consensus at the base of society about the undesirability of all weapons of mass destruction implies an intangible but paramount change in attitudes towards national security and defence. It indicates that the theory of deterrence is being seriously questioned at the popular level and that war is being seen less and less as a legitimate means of conflict resolution.

The final verdict on NFZs cannot yet be rendered. Community resistance to the arms race is fairly recent and, where it is firmly rooted, its future is still not clear. We are looking at something in the process of growth, not at the end of a process. But if humanity does have a future, one can suspect that we will owe a debt to the courage and determination of thousands of individual communities across the globe.

Addendum

On March 12, 1986, the Chicago City Council adopted a legally-binding Nuclear Free Zone Ordinance. The ordinance prohibits nuclear weapons research, production, and storage, and puts an end to city involvement in civil defence programs. Chicago is the third largest city in the United States and the first U.S. city with nuclear weapons industries to adopt NFZ legislation. Local community organizations lobbied the Council for many months before it finally reached a decision.

Because the ordinance will affect jobs and contracts in the military industries, the Council created a Peace Conversion Commission to plan for conversion of resources and facilities and to develop alternative job sources for employees of the nuclear weapons industries.

Notes

The author wishes to acknowledge the assistance of Abe Limonchik, Gerry Lipnowski, and Peter Detre in the research and preparation of this article.

1. *The New Abolitionist: Newsletter of Nuclear Free America*, Vol. 3, No. 4, (Baltimore), September/October 1985.

2. The complexity of the subject as well as the limits of time and space make it impossible to include in this discussion the special case of independent peace initiatives in Eastern Europe, but it is vital at least to state that initiatives in the Western bloc countries are not without their counterparts in the Eastern European countries and within the USSR itself. Of course, independent disarmament efforts in the Soviet Union and Eastern Europe are more difficult and involve considerably greater personal risk because they are automatically treated as civil disobedience (in contradistinction with the activities of the official peace movement which represents the positions of the central government). And while there is no question of obtaining support from local authorities, various forms of community-based resistance do exist along with the sometimes clandestine national networks of independent activists in East Germany, Hungary, Poland, Czechoslovakia, and the USSR. On this topic see for example the *Journal of European Nuclear Disarmament* and John Bacher, "The Independent Peace Movements in Eastern Europe," *Peace Magazine* (Toronto), December 1985.

3. *Disarmament Campaigns*, No. 40 (Memphis), January 1985.

4. Mary Walsh, "Nuclear Foes Fail in Efforts to Block Weapons Shipments," *Wall Street Journal*, n.d.

5. Lee Sturvidant, "Steps Taken to Ordain San Juan a Nuclear Weapons Free Zone," *Nuclear Free Zone Campaign Reports* (Baltimore, 1985), p. 33.

6. Don Skinner, "Creating Nuclear Free Communities," *Nuclear Free Zone Campaign Reports*, p. 8.

7. *A Newsletter for a Nuclear Free Japan and Pacific Asia*, International Edition (Tokyo), July 1985.

8. Rick Schreuer and Eric Segal, "Organizing for a Nuclear Free Cambridge," *Nuclear Free Zone Campaign Reports*, p. 18.

9. *Disarmament Campaigns*, No. 40.

10. Albert Donnay and Max Obuszeski, "Nuclear Free Zones and Nuclear Free Investment," *Changing Work*, No. 2 (New Haven), Winter 1985, p. 36.

11. "Excerpts from the Ruling on Referendum Over Navy Base on Staten Island," *New York Times*, 24 October 1985.

12. *Ibid.*

13. Cited in "Statement by Attorneys March 11, 1980," *Nuclear Free Zones and the Law* (Baltimore, 1984), p. 1.

14. *Ibid.*

15. Carl Eggers, "Letter to Council Members August 15, 1982," *Nuclear Free Zones and the Law*, p. 6.

16. Takeshi Araki, "Welcome Speech August 5, 1985," reprinted in Vancouver City documents regarding the First World Conference of Mayors for Peace through Inter-city Solidarity.

17. "London and Civil Defence: Why the GLC disagrees with the Government," (London, 1984).

18. Justin Schwartz, "Letter to the New Abolitionist," *Nuclear Free Zone Campaign Reports*, p. 5.

19. Steven Belling and R. Scott Kennedy, "Winning One: Santa Cruz versus Trident II," *Nuclear Free Zone Campaign Reports*, p. 37.

City of Takoma Park, Maryland

ORDINANCE No. 2703 To Declare the City of Takoma Park, Maryland A NUCLEAR-FREE ZONE

Be it ordained by the Mayor and Council of the City of Takoma Park, Maryland   12/8/83

Section 1. **Title**

This ordinance shall be known as "The Takoma Park Nuclear Free Zone Act."

Section 2. **Purpose**

The purpose of this Act is to establish the City of Takoma Park, Maryland as a nuclear free zone in that work on nuclear weapons is prohibited within the city limits and that citizens and representatives are urged to redirect resources previously used for nuclear weapons toward endeavors which promote and enhance life such as human services including child care, housing, schools, health care, emergency services, public transportation, public assistance and jobs.

Section 3. **Findings**

It is the finding of the Mayor and Council of the City of Takoma Park, Maryland, that:

- The nuclear arms race has been accelerating for more than one third of a century, draining the world's resources and presenting humanity with the ever-mounting threat of nuclear holocaust.
- There is no adequate method to protect Takoma Park residents in the event of nuclear war.
- Nuclear war threatens to destroy most higher life forms on this planet.
- The use of resources for nuclear weapons prevents these resources from being used for other human needs, including jobs, housing, education, health care, public transportation and services for youth, the elderly and the disabled.
- The United States, as a leading producer of nuclear weapons, should take the lead in the process of global rejection of the arms race and the elimination of the threat of impending nuclear holocaust.

- An emphatic expression of the feelings on the part of private citizens and local governments can help initiate such steps by the United States and other nuclear weapons powers.
- Takoma Park is on record in support of a bilateral nuclear weapons freeze and has expressed its opposition to civil defense crisis relocation planning for nuclear war.
- In view of the Nuremberg Principles, which hold individuals accountable for crimes against humanity and the illegality of nuclear weapons under international law, in adopting this ordinance this community seeks to end its complicity with preparations for fighting a nuclear war.

Section 4. **Prohibition of Nuclear Facilities**

A. No nuclear weapons shall be produced, transported, stored, processed, disposed of, or used within the city of Takoma Park. No facility, equipment, components, supplies or substance for the production, transportation, storage, processing, disposal or use of nuclear weapons shall be allowed in Takoma Park, Maryland. This prohibition shall take effect upon adoption.

B. No person, corporation, university, laboratory or institution or other entity in the City of Takoma Park knowingly and intentionally engaged in development, testing, evaluation, production, maintenance, storage, transportation and/or disposal of nuclear weapons or the components of nuclear weapons shall commence any such work within the City of Takoma Park, Maryland after the adoption of this ordinance.

Section 5. **Investment of City Funds**

The City Administrator in conjunction with the Nuclear Freeze Task Force and other interested citizen organizations shall propose a socially responsible investment policy and implementation plan, specifically addressing any investments the City may have or may plan to have in industries and institutions which are knowingly and intentionally engaged in the production of nuclear weapons or their components, and shall submit said proposal to the Mayor and Council for their consideration and implementation.

Section 6. **Eligibility for City Contracts**

The City of Takoma Park shall grant no awards or contracts for any purpose to any person, firm, corporation or entity which is knowingly or intentionally engaged in the development, research, testing, evaluation, production, maintenance, storage, transportation and/or disposal of nuclear weapons or their components. It will be the responsibility of any recipient of a city contract or award to certify by a notarized statement to city clerk that it is not knowingly or intentionally engaged in the above-defined activity. Notice of this certification shall be included in all "Requests for Proposals" issued by the City.

Section 7. **Exclusions**

Nothing in this ordinance shall be construed to prohibit or regulate the research and application of nuclear medicine or the use of fissionable materials for smoke detectors, light-emitting watches and clocks, and other applications where the primary purpose is unrelated to nuclear weapons development or fabrication. Nothing in this ordinance shall be interpreted to infringe upon the rights guaranteed by the first amendment to the U.S. Constitution or upon the power of Congress to provide for the common defense.

Section 8. **Enforcement.**

A. Any violation of this ordinance shall be a municipal infraction, the abatement of which shall be ordered by the issuance of a municipal infraction citation. The fine for each initial violation shall be $100 and for each repeat or continuing violation shall be the maximum allowable by law. Each day for which the violation exists after issuance of a municipal infraction violation shall constitute a separate offense.

B. Without limitation or election against any other available remedy, the City or any of its citizens or any other aggrieved party may apply to a court of competent jurisdiction for an injunction enjoining any violation of this ordinance. The court shall award attorney's fees and costs to any party who succeeds in obtaining an injunction hereunder.

Section 9. **Severability**

If any section, sub-section, paragraph, sentence or word of this Act shall be held unconstitutional either on its face or as applied, the unconstitutionality of the section, sub-section, paragraph, sentence or word or the application thereof; shall not affect the other sections, sub-sections, paragraphs, sentences and words of this Act, and the applications thereof; and to that end the section, sub-sections, paragraphs, sentences and words of this Act are intended to be severable.

Section 10. **Definitions**

Nuclear weapon is defined to be any device in which explosion results from the energy released by reactions involving atomic nuclei, either fission, or fusion, or both. A component of a nuclear weapon is defined to be any device, radioactive material or non-radioactive material the primary function of which is to contribute to the operation of a nuclear weapon.

Section 11. **Notification.**

A. Upon adoption of this ordinance, and annually thereafter, the Mayor and Council shall present a true copy of this ordinance to the President of the United States, to the Premier of the Union of Soviet Socialist Republics, to the ambassadors of all nations at that time possessing nuclear weapons, to the Secretary-General of the United Nations, and to the director of the International Atomic Energy Agency.

B. In addition, true copies of this ordinance shall be sent to the Governor of the State of Maryland, to the United States Senators from Maryland, to the United States Representatives representing Takoma Park, to our State Delegates and Senators, to the County Executives of Montgomery and Prince George's Counties, and to the Council members of the respective counties.

C. The Mayor and Council of Takoma Park, Maryland shall choose a town or city of approximately 17,000 inhabitants within twenty miles of Moscow, or some other city or town in the USSR as the Mayor and Council shall deem appropriate, and shall send a true copy of the Takoma Park ordinance and a letter urging the chosen town to take similar action.

Trade Unions and Peace – Lessons from Quebec

Eric Shragge and David Mandel

OUTSIDE THE VICKERS ARMS factory in east Montreal a line of peace activists hand out leaflets to passing workers as the shift changes. The activists ask the workers, who directly participate in the manufacture of the
means of death, to support their cause. The workers do not respond.
Some are openly hostile.

Two years later, on October 19, 1985, trade unionists and peace acti-
vists participate together in marches and other forms of protest across
Quebec. Their theme is "An F-18 for Peace". They demand that the cost
of one fighter be allocated for conversion and other peace projects.
Despite some problems, this marks a major step in building a co-opera-
tive relationship between Quebec trade unions, in particular the CSN
(Confédération des syndicats nationaux—Confederation of National
Trade Unions) and the peace movement.

* * *

The attitudes of peace activists towards the labour movement have been
mixed. On one hand there has often been a naive expectation that the
unions, which have traditionally tended to support progressive political
causes, would jump on the bandwagon and become a major element in a
broader social movement. On the other hand, some activists have viewed
union peace initiatives with suspicion, fearing the consequences of the involvement of large, relatively wealthy union bureaucracies alongside the
smaller, poor, and often divided peace groups.

The role of trade unions in the peace movement remains today a central issue. Workers occupy a strategic position in the economic system. It is a position that allows them to disrupt production and thus exert powerful pressure against a growing militarization of the economy. Moreover, unions in Canada and in most developed capitalist countries have been a major, and often the most consistent, force for social progress. In Quebec, the CSN in particular has been active in popular causes and, more recently, in the Sommet Populaire, has worked on an on-going basis with popular movements.[1]

But there is a lot at stake for trade union members, especially those working directly in the arms industry. At stake are their jobs and livelihood. Moreover, the economic crisis of the past decade has put unions on the defensive as they are faced with declining membership, the pressures of a growing army of unemployed, the offensive of capital, and a concerted campaign to isolate them within society. This has led unions to concentrate more exclusively on protecting what has already been won and to retreat from their broader social involvement of the 1960s and '70s, although they have also played important roles in certain limited campaigns such as the Peace Petition Caravan Campaign (PPCC).[2] But the general economic and political situation apart, the very nature of the peace movement—organizationally diffuse networks rather than bureaucratic structures—and its lack of resources have made it difficult in practical terms to establish a stable co-operative relationship with the unions.

To gain a better understanding of these problems with a view to overcoming them, this chapter focuses on the process and character of the growing involvement of one Quebec trade union federation, the CSN, in peace activities.[3]

The Growth of Concern

The CSN became actively involved in the peace question only in the summer of 1984. Until 1983 the leadership and most of the rank and file of the Quebec peace movement tended to be drawn from the English-speaking community and did not move easily in the trade union milieu. More importantly perhaps, the CSN leadership was concerned about the reaction of its members, particularly its 20,000 metallurgical workers, many of whom depended directly or indirectly on the arms industry. Fearing internal divisions, the CSN did not go much beyond general resolutions condemning the arms race.

Two independent initiatives relating to the Quebec arms industry—both eventually supported by the CSN—helped to smooth the way for a

more serious involvement. The first was a study of the Quebec shipbuilding industry and its military component. The other was a study of the
Quebec arms industry by a group of church-based activists. Both raised the
issue of jobs and the arms race and began the difficult task of seeking
alternatives, in particular, the process of industrial conversion.

The study, "Employment in Quebec Shipbuilding: When Will It
Finally Pick Up Again?", was conducted in 1983 by five researchers hired
by the CSN. Its strength lay in its analysis of a key sector of the Quebec
arms industry and its discussion of the issue of conversion as a viable alternative for an ailing economic sector. The group's mandate was to explore
ways of maintaining and increasing employment in the shipyards.

Their systematic historical survey of the industry from the initial
European settlement in Quebec uncovered a clear cyclical pattern of
development and decline: Boom periods related to war were followed by
peacetime bust. In the most recent peaceful interlude government aid and
investment in the 1960s came too late to restore the industry's competitive
position after years of stagnation and neglect. Then came the oil crisis and
the decline in Maritime transport. The authors concluded that though
political decisions linked to defence policy did periodically produce spec-
tacular recovery and expansion, the industry never experienced regular,
stable development.

A review of studies on the impact of military expenditures in the
United States led to the following conclusions for Canada:
• Military spending is far from the most effective way to create jobs
  because of its highly capital-intensive nature. As well, much of the
  technology originates in the United States and only a small proportion
  finds its way to Canada.
• Arms contracts tend to be inflationary because they are granted on a
  "cost-plus" basis.
• Investment in the arms industry does not favour growth in productivity.
• The technological innovation arising out of this industry is so specialized
  and sophisticated that it can find few civilian applications.
As for the Quebec shipyards, military spending has always been the main
source of expansion and employment but it has been incapable of producing the kind of structural reform needed that would ensure stable, civilian
production once the military orders declined.

Last but not least was the moral question: What sort of economy is it
that depends on the production of the means of destruction and death for
its health? The final chapter, "Must we earn our living by destroying?",
looked at alternatives, especially industrial conversion. The authors suggested it was possible to convince governments that conversion can create
needed jobs by producing new goods for which markets can be found.

Moreover, this would lead to savings on unemployment insurance, welfare, and the general waste of human resources. Certain companies in difficulty might find the idea appealing. Trade unions, in pressing governments for increased investment, should insist that this be used to promote civilian production aiming at full employment. More specifically, the authors suggested that the CSN choose a key industry like shipbuilding to work out a plan for conversion with the direct participation of workers and citizens.

The document concluded with recommendations that the CSN press for:
- Recognition of the right to employment, including the 35-hour week with no loss of pay, increased vacation time, voluntary early retirement with full pension, creation of a job stabilization fund, and economic development policies whose first aim is employment.
- A structural transformation of the shipbuilding industry, including the establishment of a merchant fleet, a law on Canadian content in Maritime shipping, aid to buyers of Canadian-made vessels, grants for research on Maritime transport technology, and alternative naval construction to meet specific Canadian needs (ice-breakers, for instance).
- A conversion plan to create jobs and improve the level of technology and skills at the shipyards.

This document did not receive wide distribution but by forcefully and concretely arguing that there were economically and morally attractive alternatives to jobs in the industry of death, it helped to put the peace issue on the CSN's agenda. Moreover, some of those who participated in the research were now able to put the expertise they had developed at the service of the unions and the peace movement. Through international conferences they formed links with other trade unionists working on the issue and brought the results of their work back to Quebec.

Arms Factories in Quebec—or Jobs for Peace

Out of the study on the shipbuilding industry grew a larger, more ambitious project funded by the CSN and involving researchers from the CSN as well as Montreal universities. The publication of this research helped to make the question of military industry and its conversion to civilian production a major issue on the CSN's agenda as well as on that of the Quebec peace movement.

The document, "Arms Factories in Quebec—or Jobs for Peace", has had a broad impact in Quebec. With more than 100,000 copies distributed, its design and presentation made it easily accessible to a wide range of people. Its central feature was "The Explosive Map of Quebec" which showed the location of arms factories on pull-out maps of the province and the island of Montreal. It pointed out in a direct and concrete way that Quebec was by no means a mere onlooker in the arms race. The companies identified vary in size but many were tied to the United States, either through parent companies or contracts from the U.S. military. Many were recipients of Canadian and Quebec government subsidies. On the average each Quebecer paid about $200 in taxes to subsidize them. According to the document, almost half of Canada's arms industry is in Quebec; in the Montreal area alone approximately 100,000 jobs depend on it. In 1983 Montreal area companies received 3,388 military contracts worth $1.9 billion. In the same year 40 per cent of its production, about $770 million, went for export. About 60 per cent of its exports went to the United States, mainly through the Defence Production Sharing Agreement. Under Reagan the value of these exports rocketed from $267 million in 1978 to $1 billion in 1982.

The pamphlet challenged the widely held view that arms production is a good source of job creation. It cited studies showing that the same investment in almost any other economic sector resulted in substantially more employment. It argued for alternative policies, stressing co-operative forms of production and calling for new relations with the Third World. The authors argued for conversion of military industry to production for socially useful purposes with the creation of jobs, citing efforts in England, Sweden, and elsewhere, as well as the desperate situation of Quebec's shipyards.

The publication received the support of the teachers' federation as well as the CSN, which made its support conditional on the inclusion in the editorial committee of a representative of the Metallurgical Workers' Federation. This was a measure aimed at avoiding dissension later. But although the pamphlet enjoyed considerable success in the first year, the metal workers did not make use of it.

Towards An F-18 For Peace

In the fall of 1983, at the time the pamphlet was being prepared, the Montreal peace movement was bitterly divided, and two separate demonstrations were being organized. One was planned by the Quebec Peace Council, supported by several unions and popular groups. The Peace Council, with its scarcely hidden pro-Soviet orientation, had been for many years the leading peace organization in Quebec. A second demonstration was planned by an ad hoc coalition of peace groups (initially mainly English-speaking), as well as a wide range of ecologists, feminists, and left political groups. The October 22nd Committee was openly non-aligned and supported independent peace groups in the Soviet Union and East Europe. On the morning of October 22 its human chain from the U.S. to the Soviet consulate brought together 15,000 people. Later that day, about the same number of people marched through downtown Montreal in the demonstration called by the Peace Council.

This division alienated many in the CSN. The authors of the CSN pamphlet on jobs for peace concluded that the peace movement, based largely on fear, needed a more positive program. Its agenda should not be set, directly or indirectly, by the USSR or the United States. They sought a program that would relate to Quebec and produce concrete results in the struggle for peace. Out of this discussion came the "F-18 for Peace" idea.

The campaign for a peace fund equal to the value of one of the F-18s recently ordered by the Canadian government was linked to the "dream"—a challenge to teachers and students to integrate peace and disarmament projects into the classroom and to become actively involved in a movement aimed at peace, the creation of useful jobs, and solidarity with the peoples of the Third World. The aim was to generate enthusiasm and a concrete understanding and vision of the possibilities of peace activity. The peace fund would finance the ideas that emerged.

The editorial group decided to seek union support for its project. An internal document, "Disarmament and Jobs", called on the CSN executive to move beyond pious declarations. This document presented a very broad view of the peace issue, emphasizing the role of Quebec's industry in the arms race. It also showed the relationship between militarism and the oppression of women in our society. It called on the trade union movement to take a good look at its own practices, to oppose violence, and to think in terms of an alternative model of society.

After presenting an analysis of Canada's and Quebec's roles in the nuclear and conventional arms races, the authors put forth the case for conversion, arguing that it is a union demand for socially useful jobs and that unions must begin to seek at least some control over the goods that are produced. The pursuit of such an objective would require the joint efforts of unions, technical experts, and a broad community-based movement to create a favourable political situation. Such a model has been used in Germany. Finally, instead of arming the poor countries of the Third World, we should be looking for alternative products that contribute to social and economic development.

In this context, the document presented the F-18 for Peace campaign. To be credible, the demand for a peace fund required certain conditions. First, to ask for such a sum of money (even if it was only a tiny part of the

F-18 expenditure) one had to show strong popular backing. Second, a provincial committee of representatives of the trade unions and popular groups had to be chosen to negotiate and manage the fund. Third, a committee of experts was needed to verify and analyse the benefits of the project presented. Fourth, a concentrated press campaign had to sensitize journalists and reach a large number of people. Finally, the whole project required a new form of organization.

The major features of the campaign were to be a broad program of education in schools and universities enlisting the help of teachers and professors, and a larger demonstration of all those concerned by peace and jobs. This would be a sort of referendum mandating the negotiating committee to demand the peace fund.

The project was carefully thought out, imaginative, and succeeded in highlighting Canada's and Quebec's roles in the arms race while putting forth a concrete, alternative demand. It had all the merits that the Peace Petition Caravan Campaign (PPCC), launched around the same time, lacked. But the difficult economic and political conjuncture for Quebec's unions as well as the divisions and weakness of the peace movement made the realization of this ambitious project more difficult than it might have otherwise been.

The Peace Petition Caravan Campaign, pushed by the Peace Council in Quebec, had already received the support of many unions and was being presented as the main theme for the annual fall demonstration of 1984. The non-aligned groups generally rejected or ignored PPCC, while a small number of individuals emerged to form a third, middle group. Given this situation, the CSN voted to hire two people for a couple of weeks; their task would be to find out if the F-18 for Peace was generally acceptable to the peace movement and if there were enough CEGEP and university teachers willing to take the campaign into the classrooms. When the response was positive on both counts, the CSN federation council decided unanimously to approve a budget for the campaign.

The next issue before the CSN was mobilization within its own unions. The organizers worked to avoid the usual practice in which elected and paid officials become the main channels for campaigns. These people were already over-burdened with responsibilities for everyday trade union work and the response to this type of campaign had rarely been encouraging. In addition, one of the objectives was to establish permanent committees on peace and conversion issues at various levels. The idea was to draw non-elected rank and file activists into the committees that would exist in each of the 20 federations and in each of the regions. The budget itself was broken down into expenditures by region, stressing the decentralization of the campaign, a move that was quite unusual in trade union practice.

The difficulty with this new practice was that it was new and would only develop if the local initiatives and energy were forthcoming. The committees took a long time to get off the ground. The metal workers were particularly reluctant.

By the time the campaign got underway, the value of one F-18 (including parts and training) had skyrocketed to $62 million. A committee of prominent Quebecers—Francine Fournier, former president of the Quebec Human Rights Commission, Monseigneur Adolphe Proulx, Bishop of Gatineau-Hull, and Claire Bonenfant, ex-president of the Council on the Status of Women—were selected to act as negotiators with the federal government and to oversee the disbursement of the peace fund. It was felt that 62,000 people were needed for the October 1985 demonstration to give credibility to the demand for $62 million. The campaign was supported by the entire spectrum of the peace movement, although some in the Coalition Québecoise pour le désarmement et la paix were critical of what they perceived as the top-down imposition by the CSN of its project and the Peace Council wanted to promote its own campaign against Star Wars.

The CEQ, the federation of teachers' unions, was the second of Quebec's union federations to endorse "An F-18 for Peace". But Quebec's largest federation, the FTQ (Quebec Federation of Labour, affiliated with the Canadian Labour Congress) simply did not respond even though the proposal left almost everything open for negotiation. It appeared that FTQ president Louis Laberge felt the issue was a dangerous one with benefits not so obvious given the federation's goals.[4]

October 19, 1985 saw a variety of activities across Quebec. The Montreal demonstration attracted about 5,000 people. In a turnabout from usual practice, police and journalists estimated 12,000, about the same as previous years, but the official count by organizers (conducted systematically for the first time) was the first figure. The turnout was disappointing, although spirits were high.

In Sherbrooke only 250 people demonstrated. However over 6,000 people took part in a popular referendum on the F-18 for Peace project. Ballot boxes were placed around the community and 93 per cent voted in favour. In Trois-Rivières, where a committee with representatives of the CSN, CEQ, and 30 popular and peace groups was established early, a demonstration of 1,650 people marched through the community, stopping at different landmarks.

But perhaps the most impressive action took place in the Lac St-Jean region. Instead of the traditional demonstration, a popular referendum was conducted the week before October 19, with 37 balloting locations and the mayor of Chicoutimi opening the campaign. The project received broad local media coverage and support. Approximately 15,500 voted in favour of "An F-18 for Peace". Key factors here were the construction of an F-18 testing range at Bagotville, which had created a strong resistance movement, as well as the good working relationships between the CSN and the local peace groups, which had been established early on.

The actual participation, then, fell far short of the 62,000 initially called for, reducing the impact of the day. But there were important lessons in the experience. The successes occurred where working groups combining trade unionists and representatives of peace and popular groups were established early. Moreover, as in Hull, these working groups could develop into more permanent committees. The local links forged were one of the main positive results of the campaign.

Where committees were not organized or were organized late, as in Montreal, the results were disappointing. In some federations, in particular the crucial metal workers, no committees were formed. According to Robert Cadotte, the CSN did not do its job well. The idea had been that each member bring three additional people. He, himself, spoke to about 2,000 members. Yet no more than 1,500 trade unionists came to the Montreal demonstration. This partly reflected a demobilization and a sense of powerlessness that had set in over the previous few years in face of government and media attacks, the defeat of the last public sector common front, and the rise of unemployment.

At the same time, many peace groups, especially in Montreal, did not participate as actively as they had done in the organization of the demonstrations of previous years. In part this was because the initiative had come from the CSN and it had not found a suitable means for drawing the peace groups actively into the process of mobilization. The committee in Montreal was established very late and was small.

The Future

A major task for the future is education. The dominant ideology of anti-communism and the myth of the permanent enemy have to be attacked. People must be offered a critical analysis of Canada's place in the East-West and North-South dynamic, and must be shown the links between the militarization of our culture and violence towards women. The focus of activity has to be in the local unions and at the workplace—for this, more support of the federations is a necessity.

The CSN has taken some steps in this direction, but it is only a start and there are no ready-made formulas for success. These can only be developed through further practice and learning from mistakes.

The F-18 campaign of the CSN was an important attempt to bring the issue of disarmament into the labour movement. Substantial resources were committed and the campaign was well planned with original pedagogical and mobilization strategies. It made an effort to depart from the traditional union style of centralized leadership by decentralizing its budget and devolving responsibilities to federations and to the regions. The experience gives ground for cautious optimism. The peace question is now a part of the union agenda, though progress here, as in the general population, will be slower or quicker depending on a variety of outside forces.

At the same time, peace activists should be realistic about trade union involvement in this cause. Unions are not political parties and their main agenda for the forseeable future will continue to be structured mainly by the immediate and medium-term economic interests of their members, although this defensive approach is itself proving less and less successful in the crisis.

The conflict in Montreal at Vickers illustrates the point. The federal government signed a contract with Vickers for six frigates to be built in Montreal. In the meantime, however, Vickers bought a shipyard farther up the St. Lawrence at Lauzon and shifted the contracts there. The Montreal workers have launched a "Save Vickers—Save Jobs" campaign in an effort to get the orders back. Until workers feel there is a concrete alternative, peace activists cannot expect them to put the ideal of disarmament before jobs. This does not mean, however, that the workers do not favour peace and are comfortable with the nature of their work. This was clearly shown not to be the case at a delegates' council meeting of the Metallurgical Federation devoted to this question.

The peace movement should also not expect public pronouncements by union executives to automatically mean mobilization of the base. This has very rarely been the case. The F-18 campaign shows that even strong, genuine support at the top cannot be a substitute for work in regions, federations, and locals. There is also often a tension between the bureaucratic style of organization in most trade unions (which, in Montreal at least, prevailed in the F-18 campaign) and the more open, decentralized face-to-face group and network style of the peace movement. But this can be overcome, as shown by the experience in the Lac St-Jean and Trois-Rivières areas where local committees of representatives of the trade unions and peace and popular groups worked harmoniously and have evolved into more permanent structures to continue co-operative peace work.

The issue of jobs is the most obvious link between the labour movement and disarmament. The CSN became actively involved in the cause of peace through a clear argument that the arms race is not good for jobs.

The idea of economic conversion has taken hold in union circles. The approach is mainly economic, though the need for political support is acknowledged. But even on the economic level, concrete studies are needed to solve the many technical questions involved and to prove the feasibility of the idea. Currently, the CSN and a group of Montreal researchers are undertaking such research. This project envisages the direct participation of metal workers.

But it must also be realized that conversion, as a practical proposition, is a radical demand. It challenges the legal prerogative of capital to decide what is to be produced and it cannot succeed without a major shift in the balance of political forces at all levels. Moreover, arms production will remain attractive to capital as long as the profit is there—and this will be the case as long as state orders and subsidies are forthcoming.

The issue of peace and jobs must simultaneously be approached in a more directly political way with demands for changes in government priorities away from subsidizing the arms industry to increased public investment in goods and services, such as health care, housing, day care, and education. Such an approach aims at creating a broad alliance of labour, women, youth, old people, and others, capable of changing the political balance in favour of job creation through disarmament.

Notes

1. The Sommet Populaire, an alliance of trade unionists and popular groups, established working groups on themes such as ecology, full employment, and housing. Some working groups have been more successful than others, and although the approach initially gained wide support it has not sustained the initial enthusiasm.

2. For an interesting criticism of this role see Donna Laframboise, "The Politics of the Peace Petition Caravan Campaign," *Canadian Dimension*, Vol. 18, No. 6, December 1984, and the debates that followed in Vol. 19, No. 1, March/April 1985.

3. We have interviewed Robert Cadotte, an educator employed by the CSN to work on peace issues, and have used internal and public documents of the Federation.

4. Interview with Robert Cadotte.

Fuelling the Arms Race – Canada's Nuclear Trade

Gordon Edwards

WITHOUT URANIUM, there would be no nuclear weapons. Just as slavery could not have existed without a slave trade, so the nuclear arms race could not exist without a uranium trade. And almost from the beginning of the nuclear age Canada has been the world's largest exporter of uranium.

Much of this Canadian uranium has been used to build nuclear weapons. We supplied uranium for the U.S. Manhattan Project, which produced the Hiroshima and Nagasaki bombs. For 20 years after Hiroshima, almost all of Canada's uranium was sold under military contracts for the fabrication of nuclear weapons by the United States and Britain. In 1959, 12,000 tonnes of uranium were exported (compared with 8,000 tonnes in 1984), making uranium Canada's fourth most important export that year (after wheat, wood pulp, and lumber). Almost all of this 12,000 tonnes went into bombs, even though no new military contracts for Canadian uranium had been signed since 1956.

The last shipment of uranium to the United States explicitly intended for military purposes was in 1966. The last shipment to the United Kingdom explicitly intended for military purposes was in 1972. Since that date, all uranium exported by Canada is supposed to have been used for peaceful purposes only. But because Canada has no effective control over this dangerous material once it leaves our borders, there is good reason to believe that Canadian uranium is still ending up in nuclear weapons.

Uranium has only two important commercial uses, nuclear weapons and nuclear reactors. These two uses, however, are by no means mutually exclusive. Uranium used to fuel a reactor for research or for electricity production will also produce plutonium as a by-product. The by-product plutonium in the spent fuel can be recovered and used to manufacture nuclear weapons. Thus by selling nuclear reactors and uranium around the world, Canada has helped to make widely available the essential materials from which all nuclear weapons are fabricated: uranium and plutonium.

Highly Enriched Uranium

It is often said that building an atomic bomb is not very difficult. In principle, this is true. In practice, there are many complications. It is fair to say, however, that the greatest single difficulty in building an atomic bomb lies in obtaining the strategic nuclear materials.

Natural uranium is a blend of two different types (or isotopes) called uranium-235 and uranium-238. Uranium-235 is a nuclear explosive whereas uranium-238 is not. It is not possible to build an atomic bomb out of natural uranium, because the concentration of uranium-235 (less than 1 per cent) is far too low to allow for an explosive nuclear chain reaction. In order to construct a uranium bomb it is first necessary to separate the uranium-235 atoms from the uranium-238 atoms. This separation process—called "uranium enrichment"—is difficult, expensive, sophisticated, time-consuming, and energy-intensive, because uranium-235 and uranium-238 are chemically identical and therefore cannot be separated by chemical means.

Highly enriched uranium (usually over 90 per cent uranium-235) is a strategic nuclear material because it can be used to make atomic bombs, although uranium of much lower enrichment (anything over 20 per cent) can also be used for this purpose. Low-enriched uranium (typically about 3 per cent) and natural uranium (less than 1 per cent) are not strategic nuclear materials; such materials cannot be used directly as a nuclear explosive.

The Hiroshima bomb was a simple design—called a "gun-type"— made from highly enriched uranium-235. Such a bomb is indeed easy to make. But it is very difficult to produce weapons-grade uranium-235 using present technology. Only a handful of countries in the world have this capability—the five nuclear weapons states (the U.S., UK, France, USSR, and China) and a very few others (including South Africa and Pakistan). Typically, a uranium enrichment plant covers many acres of land and uses as much energy as a large city. Such plants are large and sophisticated; they cannot be hidden from aerial surveillance. However, technological advances are gradually making uranium enrichment technologies simpler and more accessible.

Uranium-235 is the only substance occurring in nature from which an atomic bomb can be made. Plutonium-239, also a nuclear explosive, does not occur in nature but is instead created inside a nuclear reactor. Most atomic bombs nowadays are made from plutonium.

If either natural uranium or low-enriched uranium is placed inside a vessel—a nuclear reactor—and surrounded by a substance called a moderator, a sluggish chain reaction can be achieved. Energy is released by the splitting of the uranium-235 atoms. Meanwhile, some of the uranium-238 atoms are slowly transformed into plutonium-239 atoms by the absorption of stray neutrons. Thus, the uranium-238—which is *not* a nuclear explosive—is cooked into plutonium, which *is* a nuclear explosive. Because plutonium is chemically different from uranium, it is in principle much easier to obtain pure plutonium than it is to obtain pure uranium-235. The separation can be achieved chemically, in a special plant called a reprocessing plant.

The Nagasaki bomb, made from plutonium, was far more sophisticated in design than the Hiroshima bomb. It was an "implosion-type" bomb, requiring great precision in its fabrication. These are more difficult to make than the gun-type bombs, but the extra sophistication is required because a gun-type bomb made from plutonium will not make an explosion powerful enough to wipe out an entire city. Despite the greater sophistication in design, it has been shown that an implosion-type bomb can be made for about $2,000 by amateurs using materials available from commercial hardware suppliers, provided that enough separated plutonium—the essential strategic nuclear material—can be obtained. Such a home-made atom bomb would be about the size of a beachball and could fit inside the trunk of a Volkswagen.

Canada, the Indian Bomb and Several Unsavory Customers

During World War II, at a secret laboratory adjoining the University of Montreal, a team of Canadian scientists worked under the direction of European scientists to discover more efficient methods for producing and separating plutonium. This effort was part of the U.S. Manhattan Project. By 1944, Canadian plutonium research had progressed to such a point that the decision was made—in Washington, D.C.—to build the Chalk River nuclear complex in Ontario. There the world's first heavy-water reactors—and the most efficient at producing plutonium—were built. For more than two decades after Hiroshima, virtually all of the plutonium produced by the Chalk River reactors was sold to the Americans and to the British for military purposes.

A pilot reprocessing plant for separating plutonium was also built at Chalk River. Because of the deadly radiation fields surrounding the spent nuclear fuel and the complicated chemistry resulting from the presence of hundreds of radioactive contaminants, reprocessing is a difficult and dangerous operation. In 1950, a chemical explosion at Chalk River killed one man and injured three others. In 1953, the Chalk River reprocessing plant was shut down. Since then, the only reprocessing done in Canada has been on a laboratory scale.

The knowledge and experience gained by their scientists visiting Montreal and Chalk River gave both Britain and France a head-start in their own nuclear weapons programs. Indeed, all of the pilot work for the Windscale reprocessing plant in Northern England was done at Chalk River. Building on the Canadian experience, England and France quickly earned a reputation for advanced expertise in plutonium reprocessing technology, a reputation that persists to this day.

In 1956, Canada gave India a nuclear research reactor as a gift under the Colombo plan. It was a carbon copy of the NRX reactor at Chalk River and was used in exactly the same way that Canada had used the original: to produce plutonium for bombs. In the intervening years, between 1956 and 1974, Indian scientists spent a good deal of time at Chalk River, where they asked many questions about plutonium and its metallurgy, questions having no known civilian application. Canada had a reputation of not only supplying the best plutonium-producing reactors, but also having some of the best information on plutonium.

India also built a reprocessing plant with U.S. assistance and separated the plutonium from the spent fuel provided by the Canadian research reactor. In 1974 it detonated its first atomic bomb. Any other country having a supply of spent nuclear fuel can, if it chooses, do the same thing at any time, despite any promises to the contrary.

In 1969, Canada sold another carbon-copy of the NRX, this time to Taiwan. After the Indians exploded their atomic bomb in 1974, the United States discovered that Taiwan had already built a clandestine reprocessing plant. Taiwan, like India, was dangerously close to having a nuclear weapons capability. Concerned that the nuclear club maintain its monopoly over the atomic bargaining chip, the U.S. government insisted that the Taiwan reprocessing plant be dismantled or all U.S. financial and military aid would be terminated. The plant was dismantled.

Pakistan acquired a CANDU electricity-producing nuclear power plant from Canada in 1959. By 1967, then President Ali Bhutto was declaring that Pakistan would embark on a program to develop its own atomic bomb. In 1972, a team of Pakistani experts was assembled to produce a nuclear weapon. By 1975, Canada had broken off its nuclear co-operation agreement with Pakistan because the government of Pakistan would not guarantee that plutonium produced in its CANDU reactor would never be used as a nuclear explosive. Frustrated in its efforts to acquire a reprocessing plant, the Pakistani government has since embarked on a program to acquire uranium enrichment technology.

Meanwhile, in 1974 and 1975, Canada was busily negotiating the sale of CANDU reactors to Argentina and South Korea—two military dictatorships which seemed interested in developing a nuclear weapons capability. In June 1975, then South Korean ruler General Park Chung Lee told the *Washington Post* that South Korea would have to develop its own nuclear weapons if U.S. support was ever to falter. That same month, *Newsweek* reported that Park had ordered the Korean Defence Development Agency to begin research on atomic weapons. Meanwhile, Korea signed a contract to buy a reprocessing plant from France. As in the case of Taiwan, U.S. pressure was brought to bear, and Korea was forced to cancel its plans to build a plutonium separation plant.

The Argentinian generals were less dependent on the United States. They not only refused to ratify the Non-Proliferation Treaty and the Treaty of Tlatelaco (which would keep nuclear weapons out of Latin America), but they publicly stated on several occasions that they reserved the right to develop nuclear weapons whenever they chose to do so. Despite the horrendous civil rights record of the Argentinian regime, despite the obvious military intentions of the generals, despite the fact that Argentina built not one but two reprocessing plants for plutonium recovery, Canada continued to deal with Argentina and even tried to sell another CANDU reactor to them. In fact we lost money on the deal.

Bilateral Safeguards: "Good Faith"?

In justifying Canada's overseas trade in nuclear reactors and uranium, the Canadian nuclear industry and the Canadian government have leaned very heavily on the provisions of the Non-Proliferation Treaty and on bilateral safeguards whereby our nuclear trading partners solemnly promise not to use nuclear materials or technology supplied by Canada for military purposes.

It has often been noted that these safeguards are unenforceable, and that the inspection procedures and book-keeping requirements are ineffective unless there is good faith between the two parties. In other words, if a country wants to cheat, it can do so. If it wants to violate the safeguards, it can do so. If it wants to withdraw from the agreements, it can do so. And of course, even if one government decided to abide by its commitments under these bilateral agreements, there is no guarantee that all future governments will do the same. With a half-life of 24,400 years, plutonium can outlast even the most durable governments and their promises. Sooner or later, some government will choose to renege on its promises. Such a government will find itself with all the materials essential to the fabrication of a nuclear weapon.

But why would a government violate these bilateral agreements? There are many reasons. Such a government may observe that the superpowers have not lived up to their own obligations under the Non-Proliferation Treaty, which is to halt and reverse the nuclear arms race. Moreover, it is certainly not lost on any nations that the five permanent members of the United Nations Security Council are the five nuclear weapons states. The possession of nuclear weapons goes hand in hand with power and prestige in the modern world. If Ronald Reagan can justify the enormous U.S. nuclear arsenal as purely defensive, then surely the same rationale can be used by any other nation? If nuclear weapons are simply a deterrent, then why shouldn't every nation have them? On the other hand, if NATO policy is to use nuclear weapons in the event that a conflict cannot be contained by conventional means, why shouldn't other nations also have the option of using nuclear weapons as a last resort? How can a weapon or a policy be portrayed as moral for one party but immoral for another party?

The situation is further complicated by the fact that Canada has often engaged in nuclear trade with countries that have refused to sign the Non-Proliferation Treaty: Argentina, India, Pakistan, South Africa. Even when former Prime Minister Trudeau embarked upon his peace initiative, which called for a strengthening of the NPT, his government continued to sell uranium to France and tried to sell a nuclear reactor to Turkey. Both of these countries have refused to sign the NPT. It is difficult to take seriously Canada's commitment to the NPT.

It is my belief that the hypocrisy surrounding the nuclear arms race is so blatant that Canada's reliance on good faith as a means to ensure that Canadian nuclear technology will not be used for military purposes is self-deceptive and, under the circumstances, immoral.

Spent Fuel: From Chalk River to Savannah River

For decades, Chalk River Nuclear Laboratories has purchased highly enriched weapons-grade uranium from the United States for use in the NRX reactor. The spent fuel is then returned to a military plant at Savannah River, South Carolina, where the unused uranium-235 is recovered and used in military reactors to produce plutonium and tritium for

H-bombs. This traffic is in direct violation of the Nuclear Co-operation Agreement between the United States and Canada, first signed in 1955 and amended several times since. This agreement forbids the use of Canadian-supplied nuclear materials for military purposes.

When this issue was raised publicly in 1982 and again in 1984, nuclear authorities from Atomic Energy Canada Ltd. (AECL) and the federal Atomic Energy Control Board (AECB) insisted that the uranium recovered from the spent fuel be recycled for civilian purposes. This is untrue. Canadian nuclear authorities also told reporters and concerned citizens that the uranium is not Canadian property and must be returned to the United States under the terms of a leasing agreement. This is also untrue.

Canadian nuclear authorities have been quick to point out that the uranium in the spent fuel returned to the United States is actually less useful to the military program than the fresh fuel that is purchased by Canada in the first place. This is true, but irrelevant. The fact of the matter is that these shipments violate both the letter and the spirit of the Nuclear Co-operation Agreement. It sets a very dangerous precedent for our nuclear co-operation agreements with other countries around the world.

Military Use of Canadian Depleted Uranium

Canada, as the world's largest exporter of uranium, exports about 85 per cent of the uranium mined in the country. In addition, Canada has one of the largest uranium refineries in the world, located at Port Hope, Ont., and owned by the Canadian government. There are only four other uranium refineries in the world: two in the United States, one in France, and one in Britain. As a result, a great deal of uranium from South Africa and Australia comes to Canada to be refined and then re-exported.

The result is an enormous traffic in uranium, almost all of it being exported from Canada in the form of "uranium hexafluoride"—a very volatile and dangerous chemical compound. The immediate destination for this "hex mix" is invariably one of the world's uranium enrichment plants, located in the United States, France, Britain, or the USSR. These uranium enrichment plants serve a dual purpose: They produce nuclear fuel for civilian reactors (low-enriched uranium for most nuclear power plants, highly enriched uranium for some research reactors) and they produce the highly enriched uranium needed for weapons. There is no physical distinction between "atoms for peace" and "atoms for war". All the uranium hexafluoride is blended together, heated to about 125 degrees fahrenheit to turn it into a gas, and then drifted down miles of corridors so that it can be gradually enriched. Elaborate book-keeping methods are used to ensure that, "on the whole", Canadian uranium is not being used for weapons. In other words, the "deposits" of Canadian uranium going into the enrichment plant should be balanced by the "withdrawals" of enriched uranium for civilian purposes. In this way, it is argued, Canadian uranium does not contribute to the nuclear weapons program (even though it is piggy-backing on a military production line and thereby lending the entire process a peaceful veneer).

However, the deposits do not balance with the withdrawals. In order to produce one pound of low-enriched uranium (3 per cent U-235), about seven pounds of natural uranium (in the form of hexafluoride) are required. In order to achieve a higher concentration of U-235, large quantities of U-238 have to be discarded. This cast-off uranium-238 is called depleted uranium. Thus, over 85 per cent of the Canadian uranium that enters the enrichment plant ends up as depleted uranium. This material is not inspected, nor is it subject to any explicit safeguards. It is regarded as "non-strategic material". Canadian depleted uranium is not physically separated from depleted uranium of non-Canadian origin; it is all added to a common stockpile, except in the case of the USSR. When the USSR enriches Canadian uranium for a civilian customer (in Finland, Sweden, or Spain, for example) the Canadian government requires that the depleted uranium left over from the enrichment process must not remain in the Soviet Union. Thus the Soviets are forced to send the depleted uranium, along with the enriched fuel, to the customer. The reason for this is that depleted uranium does have military uses.

The two principal military uses for depleted uranium are:
(a) as "target rods" in military reactors, where the depleted uranium is used to breed the plutonium which is later used in the triggers for the H-bombs;
(b) as the outer casing of the H-bombs themselves, where the U-238 atoms are split (fissioned) by the intensely energetic neutrons produced by the fusion reaction.

About 50 per cent of the explosive power of every H-bomb is due to the fissioning of U-238 atoms in the outer jacket of depleted uranium; if that outer jacket is removed, the resulting bomb is called a neutron bomb. It produces much less blast, but gives off far more energetic neutrons. It is fair to say that half of the explosive power of the world's nuclear arsenals is due to depleted uranium. Yet this material is not considered as "strategic" material, is not inspected, and is not subject to any specific safeguards. It is routinely added to a common stockpile which is drawn upon for military or civilian purposes without regard to the origin of the uranium.

When I asked an official from Canadian External Affairs to explain why Canada is unconcerned about depleted uranium, he answered, "There is so much of this stuff lying around that it's not worth worrying about." This underscores once again the double standard implicit in the NPT and in the safeguards agreements that Canada has signed with other countries. The nuclear safeguards agreements are primarily intended to prevent nuclear have-not nations from getting their own nuclear weapons; these agreements are not intended to prevent the nuclear have nations from building as many H-bombs as they want to. Indeed, the reason why depleted uranium is considered non-strategic material is because it cannot be used to make a bomb unless one already knows how to make the plutonium triggers for H-bombs. Thus depleted uranium is considered to be of little use to a nuclear have-not nation, except as a target material for breeding plutonium.

Because uranium is about twice as heavy as lead, it has certain other non-essential uses. For example, it can be used as a counter-weight in airplane gyroscopic systems. It can also be used as a coating for ordinary bullets to make them much more penetrating. This latter application is being actively pursued by several companies in Canada. Because depleted uranium is a non-strategic material, it is much easier to acquire than highly enriched uranium or separated plutonium, or even reactor fuel.

In 1981, four Israeli jets bombed the OSIRAK nuclear reactor near Baghdad in Iraq. The Israelis claimed that the Iraqis were planning to build an atomic bomb, using plutonium produced in the reactor after separating it from the spent fuel in an underground laboratory. The reactor was to be fuelled with highly enriched uranium supplied from France, but France argued that this strategic nuclear material would be carefully accounted for by means of on-site inspection to ensure that Iraq would not use the weapons-grade uranium for weapons purposes.

But there is a dangerous loophole in this system of safeguards. The Iraqis could, when the inspector is not around, insert target rods made of depleted uranium into the reactor, allowing them to soak up neutrons and produce plutonium. These target rods could be withdrawn before the inspector returned, thereby breeding the plutonium needed for a nuclear weapon without anyone being the wiser.

As it happens, just about a year before the reactor was bombed, Eldorado Nuclear Limited was involved in a bizarre transaction involving depleted uranium in a deal set up by a West German firm. U.S. authorities were extremely curious as to why Eldorado was engaged in producing metal rods of depleted uranium for some unspecified customer overseas. Investigation showed that the ultimate destination for the depleted uranium rods was Iraq. U.S. officials blew the whistle, and the AECB stopped the transaction.

This example simply illustrates the possibilities that exist for bypassing the existing safeguards. Slugs of depleted uranium could also be used in a CANDU reactor to breed plutonium when the inspectors aren't around, using the CANDU's unique feature of on-line refuelling. In many ways, this would be simpler than recovering the plutonium from the CANDU fuel itself, although the latter option is also a possibility.

Economic Considerations

Nuclear power has yet to demonstrate its economic feasibility: Not a single vendor of nuclear power plants anywhere in the world has yet made a profit. The nuclear power industry would never have come into existence had it been left to private capital. It was essentially a civilian spin-off of a multi-billion dollar military program. In the early literature of the subject, there is much talk of making use of the waste heat from plutonium-production reactors—hence the concept of electricity generation as a by-product of plutonium production.

It is clear that if government subsidies were withheld from the nuclear industry, it would collapse. It seems equally clear that the only rationale for building the Darlington reactors in Ontario or a second Point LePreau reactor in New Brunswick is to keep the nuclear industry alive. Neither province is short of electricity; in fact both provinces have substantial surpluses. Nor do the U.S. customers have a shortage of electricity; they are also in a surplus situation. Moreover, alternative energy analyses indicate that non-nuclear approaches to the problem of satisfying our future energy needs are more economically sound than a reliance on nuclear power.

The economic benefits of uranium mining are also highly dubious. Uranium mining produces large quantities of dangerously radioactive tailings which, all parties agree, must not be left abandoned on the surface of the earth. Canada already has about 100 million tons of these uranium tailings. It is going to cost hundreds of millions, if not billions of dollars, to dispose of these toxic wastes, which have an effective half-life of 80,000 years. Yet the mining companies are under no financial obligation to dispose of these wastes in a permanently satisfactory fashion.

At present, uranium fetches about U.S. $25 per pound. At Elliot Lake, one ton of ore will scarcely produce two pounds of uranium. If the cost of waste disposal is $30 per ton or more, as seems likely, then uranium mining is uneconomic and should be stopped.

As a footnote it is important to realize that the medical and industrial uses of radiation do not depend in any essential way on the uranium trade.

If the uranium trade were completely halted, the use of X-ray machines would be completely unaffected. Moreover, radioisotopes used in medicine, agriculture, and industry do not require a nuclear reactor for their production. They can be produced in cyclotrons and in various other types of accelerators.

Ending the Arms Trade

Technically it would not take much to starve the nuclear arms race. It only requires ending its food supply: the two so-called strategic materials from which nuclear weapons are fabricated, highly enriched uranium and separated plutonium. Indeed, if enrichment plants and reprocessing plants were outlawed around the world, it would not be possible to produce the strategic nuclear materials from which new nuclear weapons could be made. These plants are so large and conspicuous that it is quite possible to verify by aerial surveillance that such plants are being built or operated anywhere in the world. This would put an end to the traffic in strategic nuclear materials.

It is then technically possible to remove the strategic nuclear material from the existing warheads and render them useless for nuclear weapons use. In the case of highly enriched uranium, this would involve mixing the U-235 back in with the U-238. In the case of plutonium, it would require mixing the separated plutonium back in with the high level radioactive wastes. These materials would still exist, but they would be unavailable for weapons use. Moreover, these materials could not be made available for weapons use without building and operating an enrichment plant or a reprocessing plant.

Because of the development of new technologies, such as the laser enrichment of uranium, the above measures may not be sufficient in the long term to prevent the construction of nuclear weapons. I therefore believe that the only real security lies in abolishing the uranium trade altogether. This, of course, means foregoing nuclear power as an energy source. Given what we know about the disadvantages of nuclear power, this may not be a sacrifice at all, but a blessing. Even if it *were* somewhat of a sacrifice, it seems a small price to pay to keep alive the dream of a nuclear-disarmed world—a world that will remain liveable for our children and our grandchildren.

The Women's International Peace Conference – A Report

Marion Kerans

VOICE OF WOMEN CANADA was alarmed and incensed—alarmed by the breakdown of the Geneva negotiations in November 1983 and incensed that women were excluded from disarmament negotiations. We believed that if women were present negotiations would be a meaningful process. We were also disturbed that our government had done little to promote Canadian women's involvement in international affairs despite the themes of the UN Decade for Women: equality, development, and peace.

Insisting that women have a contribution to make to disarmament negotiations, VOW organized a coalition of national women's organizations to co-sponsor an international women's peace conference. The title itself—"The Urgency for True Security: Women's Alternatives for Negotiating Peace"—gave notice that women intended to define what "true security" meant. By giving large grants to the conference, the federal government (through the Disarmament Division, Department of External Affairs, and the Secretary of State) acknowledged the support of Canadian women for Voice of Women.

At the initial meeting of the Coalition of Canadian Women's Groups—International Peace Conference, women from 26 women's organizations set the conference goals. We would define true security; analyse the current status of international negotiations; trace the links between all forms of violence and the threat of war; share skills, experiences, and ideas on alternative ways to resolve conflict and build trust; explore how the application of these alternatives could reduce present levels of hostility; and promote ways to transfer global resources from arms to development.

To prepare for the international conference over 3,000 Canadian women of different racial, religious, political, and economic backgrounds were involved in 14 regional and local conferences. Many of these women were new to the peace movement but were deeply concerned about the possibility of nuclear war and the threat to human survival. The mini-conferences were an example of flexible and co-operative organizing among women from many different groups to express women's alternatives. One hundred of these women became delegates to the international conference.

Meanwhile, the coalition was inviting women's groups and women in the peace movement to endorse the conference goals. There were 37 groups that did so and each of these was invited to send a delegate. To this grassroots base we added 70 resource women from 33 countries. These women, besides demonstrating a commitment to international peace and security issues, had all taken creative approaches to conflict resolution, and had experience in achieving non-violent solutions to situations of confrontation.

Before the conference, planners asked all participants to discuss with women at home what made them feel secure, what issues could never be compromised and where compromises could be found, what national governments should do or have done to establish successful negotiations, and what major problems are experienced in each country. In addition, resource women were asked to identify which structures and policies needed to be changed and what women could do (including how women might get into positions to negotiate and how they might negotiate differently).

The conference was held for four days in June 1985 at Mount Saint Vincent University, Canada's only women's university. The extensive preparation for the conference helped to ensure that its participants would reflect the perceptions and judgements of a great many women throughout the world. It brought together a broad spectrum of grassroots and resource women: 350 women from 33 countries, including 55 foreign women and 25 Canadians from visible minorities. There were women representing every continent as well as an assortment of political ideologies.

Women's View of Security

For the first three days of the conference, speakers, panel discussions, and small group workshops concentrated on issues of security, negotiations, and the effect of the arms race on women. As might be expected, participants had many different ways of expressing what security meant to them, depending on their individual and collective situations in their own countries. Freedom from fear and freedom from dominance and oppression were integral to every woman's view.

We nodded in recognition when Margareta Inglestam of Sweden said she felt secure when she watched her children sleeping peacefully at night and we were moved when she said that her daughter longed to know if it was safe to bring a new baby into the world. Vilma Nunez de Escorcia from Nicaragua described how the women of her country confronted death and destruction from the U.S.-backed *contras*; they know that their security is not a gift that will come from the outside. Ursula Franklin of Toronto pointed out that the word security came from the biblical exhortation to fear not, but now is used by governments to sell ideas and institutions that produce fear. What is peddled as security, she said, is not *our* security, but the security of territory and of profit.

Eva Norland, Norwegian leader of international peace marches to Paris, Moscow, and Washington, talked about two perceptions of security. The first is the traditional way, to assemble equipment and become at least as militarily strong as the adversary. But in a nuclear age the search for perfect security sooner or later comes to mean total insecurity. The second perception of security is to see the interdependence of the world's people and of humanity and nature. "True security", she said, "is to care for everything that we have in common, first of all our whole globe. True security is to protect the people of all countries. It is to guard all aspects of life. It is to feel solidarity with all parts of the globe."

Reappropriating the concept of security was a major achievement of the conference. Hilka Pietilla of Finland remarked, "The military people have gained a decisive victory when they have taken over or 'occupied' the territory of language in which [peace] negotiations are conducted."

Breaking the culture of silence was another bond among many women at the conference. Josephine Mandamin from White Dog reserve spoke for many when she said, "I want to tell you that I am frightened speaking to you because basically I am a shy person. But when something threatens my future resources—the young children of White Dog and my grandkids—nothing else matters. I want the kids of White Dog to have a chance of security."

The Effect of the Arms Race on Women

The arms race represents an enormous waste of human and material resources. Delegates from Argentina, Belize, the Philippines, Ethiopia, Lebanon, Chile, Tahiti, French Melanesia, and our Natives, Metis, and Canadians of visible minorities emphasized the links between disarmament and development, or better, between the arms race and underdevelopment.

Agnes Aidoo, originally from Ghana but now working in Addis Ababa at the UN's African Training and Research Centre for Women, described the distorted pattern of African development:

> Africa is caught in a vicious circle of external indebtedness, oppression, and militarism fanned by the arms race. We produce what people do not consume at home and then import what people need to eat. The stress on export production takes away resources from local food production and from industries based on agricultural products that the people could grow and cultivate. The result is constant hunger and unemployment. Tensions grow, force is used to suppress opposition. Governments can do this because they import arms. The trading partners are quite happy with this because their biggest interest is stability. When the going gets too rough one group of soldiers is given outside support to remove the government and put itself in.
>
> Defence expenditure is a major form of consumption in Africa. Whom are we defending ourselves from? More than one half of the developing countries spend more money on arms than on food and agriculture, health and education. The net result is either no development, very poor development, or very slow development on the continent. Then the people are preoccupied with sheer survival or running away from death. It affects women profoundly. Women are not participating in the decisions that make these priorities. There is a painful need for us to find ways and means to determine the priorities of our societies.

Donor countries virtually ignore the fact that Africa spends more money on military expenditures than it receives for aid. Agnes Aidoo challenged Canadian women to act because we are in a relatively stronger position to influence our government than African women are to influence theirs.

Workshop after workshop called on the Canadian government to demilitarize the North. To paraphrase Ursula Franklin, Canada is in a perfect geographic position to keep the two superpowers apart just as a mother would two warring children, and to act as a peacemaker and mediator. The militarization of the North that oppresses Native peoples and makes us an accomplice in the creation of a world hegemony for one of the superpowers is intolerable for Canadians. Workshops urged all Canadian women to work actively for the Canadian government to withdraw from NORAD, to oppose Star Wars, and to cease all nuclear weapons testing in the North. As well, women from Newfoundland and Labrador protested the increasing militarization of Labrador for NATO purposes and the disregard for local effects on the environment.

What's Wrong With Present Negotiations?

Maria Nzomo of Kenya raised three main objections to present disarmament negotiations. They are based on the assumption that the greatest threat to peace in the world today is nuclear weapons, ignoring the very immediate threat to peace for more than two-thirds of humanity by the crisis of underdevelopment. Secondly, except for the UN Committee on Disarmament, all major peace negotiations have been confined to the two superpowers. Finally, there is a tendency to underestimate the magnitude of armed conflicts in Third World countries and a failure to challenge the military buildup of conventional and, in some cases, nuclear weapons. This buildup will be harder to control at a later date if the underlying economic and political causes are not dealt with now.

Joanna Miller of Saskatoon recommended a new approach to all disarmament negotiations:

> First, Western nations including Canada must understand that survival is the issue—not jobs, not profits, not being a good guy, but survival. Secondly, Western nations including Canada should exert every pressure possible to change American perceptions: to bring them to recognize that one-upmanship in the nuclear age is suicidal and that in the nuclear age, security is possible only within a system where everyone's security is guaranteed. The more the superpowers threaten each other's security, the more they undermine their own. Thirdly, Canada and other middle powers should exert every effort to change American policies. A place to start would be with the restoration of civility between the superpowers and a return to normal relations in all aspects of life—trade, cultural relationships, scientific exchanges, etc. There should be a strengthening of the role of the United Nations in crisis management and regional conflict resolution, such as the Contadora process [in Central America]. But most importantly, efforts must be made to persuade the U.S. administration of the need for genuine progress in arms control.

Women at the conference saw military solutions to political problems as the main impediment to peace. The question was never which weapons should be eliminated or reduced. The question was the use of weapons and military force itself. Although armed struggle in wars of liberation was never condemned, we admitted that the use of force results in further recrimination and the circle of violence continues. While women from the developed countries thought that nuclear proliferation was the greatest threat to peace and security, women from the poor countries saw starvation and military governments as the greatest threats. Together we saw militarism as the ultimate expression of a patriarchal system that is endangering the survival of all our children. Negotiating non-violent solutions to political problems is in every country's national interest. We refused to accept that disarmament negotiations could be divorced from the causes of war: poverty, oppression, violation of human rights, racism, and sexism.

Bringing It Together

As a draft conference statement was read on the final morning, women cheered our consensus. But we were not to leave this conference without experiencing our own internal negotiating process. Many delegates were persuaded that we could not leave without showing support for the separate struggles for peace and social justice that women are engaged in around the world. They wanted to have resolutions passed that addressed these concerns. On the other hand, some women felt that our task was to address only the common alternatives and priorities which women wanted to bring to disarmament talks, and to propose ways to create new policies and structures. Some delegates expressed concern that time did not permit an adequate review of the many issues listed and that some unrepresented countries would not have their own conflicts addressed.

Finally, we agreed on a new method to deal with the proposed resolutions. We would call them affirmations. Time was extended and each affirmation was reviewed. When we came upon differing proposals, such as the problems presented by the Israeli/Palestinian situation or the status of Native women in Canada, we indicated our support for each affirmation with the recommendation that further negotiations between women from both sides needed to be held. Commenting on this process, Martha Gooding stated,

> Some people, it is true, had hoped for a different product—a new structure to be developed or a new way of negotiating to spontaneously emerge. If we want to have non-violent solutions (and we all say we do) we must make certain that we don't commit the violence of silencing people before they have a chance to speak, or relegating their vital concerns to the "less important" category, while we get on with our own agenda. People can only feel represented by such things as a conference statement if they feel that statement incorporates their specific concerns. Otherwise those whom the statement is supposed to represent will feel they have had a "solution" imposed on them, and imposing solutions is not what negotiating peace is all about.

In the end not only was there consensus on the conference statement but also the delegates produced 73 affirmations directed to 16 countries along with a seven-page list of action plans. One novel idea was the notion of "girlcotts", where we would use our economic power to buy products from such countries as Nicaragua and New Zealand. We called for a women's conference on the Middle East (to include the PLO), and for the release of specific women political prisoners in South Africa, the Philippines, El Salvador, and England. We urged the United Nations to establish a list of women experts able to participate in conflict resolution. We further demanded that women lawyers and doctors always be included in teams investigating allegations of torture, and conditions in prisons, detention centres, refugee and prisoner-of-war camps. We called on Canadian women to provide increased material support to South African and Namibian refugee women and their families.

A Women's International Network for Peace

The solidarity between women from developing countries and those of us from developed countries was the most hopeful sign of the conference. As Gloria Steinem once said, "Women are in themselves a Third World nation. Our conditions, status, lack of power make us a Third World nation in any society." Simone Wilkinson of the Women's Peace Camp at Greenham Common, England, summed up the feelings of many women when she said, "Women are a nation in exile behind their own borders."

As women we refuse to admit powerlessness. Our conference poster showed a young woman of indeterminate racial origin. The caption read: "No Victim I / Victime? Pas Moi!"

One of the outcomes was a petition to be circulated and then presented to the United Nations asking that women be given the status of a separate nation, with representation on all UN bodies. It states that women are a nation in exile and that we are systematically excluded from all the political and economic power structures of all nations. It states that the skills of women are not valued or used by any government: those skills of caring and co-operative behaviour that nurture the world.

A drafter of the conference statement, Luanne Armstrong, later reported: "For the five days of the conference the reality of the women's world existed within the reality of the whole world. The women of the conference understood how connected are the problems they face, from uranium mining in Saskatchewan to atomic bomb testing in the Pacific, from the sale of war toys to the building of Star Wars. From Lebanon to South Africa to Nicaragua, women share a common understanding that breaks down the barriers of nationality and race."

Conference Statement

- We 350 women of the world community, from 33 countries, meeting at the Women's International Peace Conference in Halifax, Canada, June 5-9, 1985, affirm the overwhelming need and desperate urgency for peace, which we believe is both the process we live and the goal for which we work.

- At this conference, women from diverse racial, cultural, ethnic and political backgrounds representing different sides of conflict areas, came together as a living example of women negotiating peace. Some of us compromised our own safety to make this commitment.

- Although women's voices have not been heard and women have not participated equally in peace negotiations or in formulation of the institutions and the cultural fabric in which we live, we are more than half the world's population; we do have power; and we are shaping it for peaceful living.

- We reject a world order based on domination, exploitation, patriarchy, racism and sexism. We demand a new order based on justice and the equitable distribution of the world's resources.

- We condemn militarism. Militarism is an addiction that distorts human development, causing world-wide poverty, starvation, pollution, repression, torture and death. Feeding this habit robs all the world's children and future generations of their inheritance.

- We all live in the shadow of the threat of nuclear war. We demand an end to research, testing, development, and deployment of all weapons of mass destruction, to the militarization of space and to all forms of violence. As a first step, we call for a comprehensive test ban treaty.

- We support the rights and the efforts of all peoples to self-determination and to freedom from military and economic intervention. As an example, we cite Nicaragua as a new kind of society, and as a symbol of hope which must be allowed to live.

- We will continue to communicate and join with women all over the world in our struggle for peace. As a result of this conference, we are developing a world-wide women's peace network. Our first act has been to pledge our vigilance in monitoring the ongoing safety of our sisters who are at risk as a result of attending this conference.

- We are committed to acting globally, nationally, locally and individually for peace. We will not compromise our commitment to the survival and healing of this planet.

- We affirm the right of every human being to live with dignity, justice and joy.

June 9, 1985

The Movement and the Levers of Power

Dr. Paul Cappon

A FUNDAMENTAL ASSUMPTION concerning the nature of political power in Canada has determined much of the strategy of the movement for nuclear disarmament. That assumption rests on the observation that members of parliament are decision-makers in Western parliamentary systems. Thus, if the disarmament movement wishes to alter Canadian participation in the nuclear arms race, it must gain access to the levers of political power, to its elected representatives. Strategies such as letter campaigns, demonstrations, and direct representation to members of parliament are based on the possibility of persuading government leaders to adopt rational policies.

But what if the disarmament movement is mistaken? What if the decisions to participate in the nuclear arms race are not made in parliament? What if we are incapable of adapting the normal political process to establish peaceful human relations? This is an issue clearly worth examining: It would be unfortunate to continue to expend great energies on those tactics which might not bring better access to the levers of power.

My own orientation has been to work closely with Canadian politicians to encourage nuclear rationality. This experience suggests that the usual political process may not offer a real opportunity for substantial alteration of Canadian support for military escalation.

The power structure is such that its positions regarding issues of war and peace cannot easily be shifted. It is not likely that a segment of the Canadian population can convince its political leaders to adopt an activist consciousness of the threat of the nuclear arms race and their responsibility to develop an autonomous Canadian policy.

For one thing, fact and objectivity matter hardly at all in East-West relations, so that it would be difficult to bring Canadian politicians to such a consciousness through rationality. Secondly, the internal political world of most politicians is such that their aspirations are almost more important than their own survival. Putting it another way, in this desperately internal political life, political survival *is* survival.

What this implies is that a change in the attitude of power towards our survival will not occur gradually. It will instead require one event or a distinctive series of events that would have the effect of demasking the hollowness and concentrated self-interest of many of those who govern.

In addition it is important to recognize that the levers of power concentrated by the political structure are not integrated as tightly as one might expect. In talking to politicians and government officials—to people supposedly in power—I have been surprised by the influence of chance and circumstance in the adoption of policy. The power structure appears to be something of a paper tiger. Its appearances are formidable because of its seeming inflexibility and its immense capacity to deflect criticism, together with its naked use of power when this appears necessary to defeat the peace movement. However, because of the very looseness of its interconnections, the ideological basis for the arms race could fold like a house of cards when appropriately challenged.

Experts and Babes

In July 1982 I participated in the 25th Commemorative Pugwash Conference on Science and World Affairs. The International Pugwash Conference on Science and World Affairs was begun on the initiative of Bertrand Russell and Albert Einstein, who, in the mid-1950s, were concerned about the nuclear arms race. Together with other eminent scientists and philosophers, they signed a manifesto which led eventually to the formation of the International Pugwash Movement for Science and World Affairs. The first conference was held in Pugwash, Nova Scotia because it was the home town of industrialist Cyrus Eaton, who provided financing. The movement has grown substantially since 1957 and now has chapters in over 40 countries and includes many prominent scientists, social scientists, and diplomats.

The 25th Commemorative Pugwash Conference was held in Pugwash for the first time since 1957. Surviving members of the original Pugwash group were invited, as well as 29 other participants. Around the table sat several Nobel Prize winners, including Linus Pauling and Garcia Robles, the 1982 Mexican winner of the Nobel Peace Prize for his work on a Swedish-Mexican resolution for the nuclear freeze. Prominent scientists and diplomats included Joseph Rotblatt from the UK, Bernard Feld from the United States, Inga Thorsson from Sweden, and Sir Mark Oliphant, the Australian physicist who worked on the original atomic bomb and has been in the nuclear disarmament movement ever since.

Apart from the sheer pleasure of working for a weekend with such distinguished people, my overwhelming impression from this experience was one of helplessness. Their feelings were no different from those of people in the street. Consider this: Individuals, some of whom are the most recognized authorities in their field, all of whom are respected as well for an active, broad participation internationally in human affairs, felt, like the rest of us, as children who had no influence, as voices simply not being heard.

Many ordinary persons feel themselves helpless and inadequate. They rationalize their inactivity by declaring that, as ordinary persons, they have no influence. But how might this change if they were aware that those who are perceived as having influence feel equally helpless? Indeed, for me, the main conclusion of the Pugwash Conference was that its participants could do little more than hope for the success of a broadly based international disarmament movement. In other words, the only hope was that ordinary people could succeed where the elite of science, social science, and diplomacy had failed.

This is not defeatism or passivity. It is a simple recognition that no individual elite can shift, even moderately, the implacable power structure which leads us to our extinction. The power structure is impervious to rational argument and uninterested and unimpressed by the opinions of the great thinkers.

The lesson I drew from this experience was that we cannot look to any elite, whether scientific, diplomatic, or intellectual, for fundamental leadership in the peace movement. While we wait for that leadership they wait for the rest of us. In the 1980s there is no influence or power in genius. The disarmament movement depends solely on hard work and moral courage.

We touch here, then, on my first conclusion, that fact and rationality are not important factors in the conduct of East-West relations or in the political systems of those who govern them. Power is what is at issue here, power to be used or misused and abused. And, in the current pre-war phase of barbarism through which we are going, power has nothing to do with rationality. This is why the intellectual elite appears to me to be as lost as babes in the woods: It is a new experience for them. If this conclusion is accepted, at least in part, it means that the disarmament movement will not succeed by appeals to the rationality of those who control the levers of power.

In the physician disarmament movement, Helen Caldicott, the former president of Physicians for Social Responsibility United States, has often been criticized for her rather emotional approach to the question of nuclear war. The grounds for the criticism have been that such an approach would tend more to alienate than to persuade. My conclusion suggests that this criticism is unfounded. There is, of course, much room for rational explanation and education. However, because of the way in which power is now exercised, fundamental policy change will not be brought about through rational dialogue.

Canadian Members of Parliament

Perhaps the most important strength of the power structure in relation to nuclear policy is its very intangibility, its evasiveness, the difficulty of identifying and seizing it. We know that the U.S. president and his chief advisors have power. We know that the Canadian prime minister has power, as do some of his advisors. But does anyone else have power? Do members of parliament and cabinet ministers, for example, have power? The question obviously is a fundamental one if we wish to influence the power structure. We must know about the attitudes of those who at least are perceived to have power. Most will agree that members of parliament and cabinet ministers are perceived by the public as being powerful.

From interviews with some 30 or 40 members of parliament and cabinet ministers on the subject of Canada's participation in the nuclear arms race, I find that they fall into three general categories regarding their receptiveness to the nuclear disarmament position. The first category is composed of those members of parliament who are very receptive to nuclear disarmament positions. Most of them have, to varying degrees, some independent knowledge and assessment. The second category is composed of those who appear ideologically incapable of thinking about the issue in any serious or rational manner. This ideological incapacity is derived from a Cold War mentality.

The third category is the largest and constitutes that mass of politicians whom the disarmament movement would presumably want to influence. These people's views are more complex because they are influenced by shifting factors and by political self-interest. The chief characteristics of this group are rapid changeability, ignorance of the issues, inability or unwillingness to find independent or objective information, concentration on the internal political world, and absence of strong moral, philosophical, or political beliefs regarding this set of issues.

Typically, this type of politician is generally worried about the nuclear arms race, particularly if he or she has a family. Information tends to be supplied by the Department of External Affairs or the Department of National Defence, which often get the information from U.S. sources. This is particularly true of information concerning the relative military strength of East and West, nuclear arms buildups, and nuclear arms negotiations. Much of this is misinformation provided by U.S. authorities precisely to influence allied Western politicians. Other major sources of information for members of parliament include U.S. publications such as *Time* magazine. Very few of these politicians consult or have even heard of independent observers such as the Stockholm International Peace Research Institute. When they are presented with objective information from independent sources, such as SIPRI, they tend to view this information with a mixture of interest and suspicion. This suspicion is related to the independence of the information. When the information is presented by persons whom they consider reliable, such as representatives of Physicians for Social Responsibility Canada, they tend to be willing to look at it.

These politicians are generally unreserved about their fear regarding U.S. reprisal in the case of any autonomous Canadian positions on important foreign policy or military matters. They will admit quite openly their fear of economic reprisal. What this means is that, even if they accept the rationality of a disarmament position, they may still be unwilling to act. This is particularly true since the nature of their occupation provides them only with limited concentration. Today they may have been concerned about the nuclear arms race. Tomorrow it may be the Shriners' Circus.

This is to say that their main concern is still their own political survival and their own political world. In this world, relative importance is determined not by the absolute significance of an issue but by the impact of that issue on their own political careers. No political advantage can be gained by being perceived as an alarmist by members of one's own party or by the public in general. This is why certain politicians have been quickly put out into the margins of their own party. One must appear to be a moderate even if that moderation is not in keeping with a rational position regarding the issue.

How then can this important category of politicians be influenced? It is very difficult. There are ideological constraints; there are constraints posed by the information provided by the U.S. public relations machine; there is a lack of concentration dictated by the political world; there is the fact that these politicians are easily intimidated by U.S. lobbyists, especially regarding economic issues. Finally, any progress made with these individuals is apt to be of short duration because they tend to go on to other questions. In Canadian politics, it is a liability to be perceived as a one-issue person.

What then is the task with respect to this political group? One important task is to give these politicians support at every possible opportunity, so that they may be encouraged to develop moral courage, that courage which is necessary to face possible intimidation. Every small action which they take in the right direction must be applauded. In addition, they need to be encouraged to develop their own independent sources of information. Provision of this information is an important role for nuclear disarmament activists.

Finally, they need personal contact with disarmament activists in order to take them out of their own unreal internal political world. That world, rather like a hospital ward, is a realm unto itself; many of those within it have insufficient grasp of the real world outside. Once they develop this grasp, through contact with human beings in that outside world, they become more open to perception of the nature of the threat, and perhaps also to rationality as an approach to East-West relations and the nuclear arms race.

At the Table with Trudeau

To this point I continue to beg the question: Where is the locus of power? How does one locate the levers? In January 1984, during his peace initiative, Prime Minister Trudeau held two "peace luncheons" at 24 Sussex Drive, to which he invited several representatives of the nuclear disarmament movement in Canada. I was present at one of these meetings. During the lunch each of us had an opportunity to express our views to Mr. Trudeau and to hear his extended reply. Each of us developed a different theme, but what we had in common were views contrary to those currently held by the government. Mr. Trudeau did not disagree with a single one of our views. Yet, although he could not disagree with them intellectually, he made it clear he did not believe it was possible to adopt them as government policy. How is this possible? How could there be such a gap between the private views of a prime minister and his public positions as reflected by government policy? Or to put it another way, if the prime minister cannot modify Canadian nuclear policy, then who can? Again, this is an example of the evasiveness of the political structure and the difficulty even of finding out whom we must persuade.

In this context, when one considers appropriate disarmament strategies, the utility of mass demonstrations must be re-assessed. In such a loose power structure, in which no one is ever sure where the locus of power resides, one may surmise that demonstrations, taken alone, have very little effect on political decision-making regarding the nuclear arms race. The huge demonstrations in the United Kingdom and West Germany have adequately demonstrated that. The principal significance of these demonstrations is that they give a means of access to political leaders for the leadership of the disarmament movement. And that is perhaps all they accomplish.

Keeping Peace on the Defensive

An important tactic employed by the politically powerful is to keep the peace movement at bay. We all are aware of tactics such as misinformation, propaganda, legalism and co-optation. But we tend to neglect this other overall guiding principle in the antidisarmament armamentarium of militarism, of keeping the peace movement continually on the defensive. The government has a tendency to continually move on from one military initiative to the next. The disarmament movement is continually reacting to the most recent. Meanwhile, the previous five or six initiatives have been concretized, put in place. In short, they become irremovable. An obvious example from current experience is the way in which the Star Wars program has almost made people forget about the on-going deployment of Pershing and Cruise missiles in Europe. Another is the MX missile. It may be that the exponential nature of nuclear arms aggression is overwhelming the peace movement with detail.

In this regard it is also interesting to note with respect to these hypotheses the comparative value of authoritative versus non-authoritative statements on East-West relations.

In 1983 Brian Mulroney was elected leader of the Progressive Conservative party and was running for a seat in parliament in Nova Scotia. Together with three other representatives of the disarmament movement I met with him during the election campaign in order to ascertain his views on this issue and to give him ours. Mulroney was provided with authoritative independent information, which he accepted to study.

When we left the meeting with Mr. Mulroney, we were met by Elmer McKay, who had given up his seat in that riding so Mulroney could run. (McKay became the riding's M.P. again in the 1984 election, and was appointed Canada's solicitor-general in the new Mulroney government.) McKay remarked to us, "I hope that you decided to send Cruise missiles through the Kremlin windows"—a comment clearly not entirely meant as a joke.

Unfortunately, such views have more influence on political decision-makers than either the leadership of the peace movement or mass demonstrations themselves. They are closer to the levers of power. Expressed another way, it appears immaterial that a majority of Canadians might be against current nuclear policy. As long as the power structure believes it can get away with its current policy, it will continue no matter what public opinion appears to say. In the case of Elmer McKay, it is interesting to note that Mr. Mulroney named him senior policy advisor shortly after the election of the Conservative government. It is this kind of aggressiveness on the part of the power structure that helps to place disarmament activists on the defensive.

In summary, I am not able to locate the power structure with precision. It appears to be both intransigent and diffuse. These are its strengths, and, I believe, also its weaknesses. I believe, for example, that faced with a massive campaign by a people who refuse to recognize the legitimacy of any government which continues an irrational nuclear policy, the institutional support for the policy structure would collapse overnight. Its levers of power would be unveiled as hollow. The apparent diffuseness of the power structure that surrounds these policy determinations would allow persons connected with it to withdraw diplomatically and quickly.

There is also a glimmer of hope possible through that one event which will precipitate a series of events which could in turn lead to survival. This, for example, is the significance of the case of New Zealand: the possible domino effect. Just give us several New Zealands and the chances for a reversal of the situation grow substantially stronger.

Bypassing the Political Process

The foregoing anecdotal observations and reflections lead to a conclusion that the nuclear disarmament movement will not per se make adequate progress through a political process that will attempt to control and turn to its own advantage every step until the end, using whatever means are available to it. Politicians, public servants, and other participants in the political process are either relatively helpless or simply ideologically disinclined towards nuclear disarmament.

It appears to me that a disarmament strategy more likely to achieve ultimate success is one that places emphasis on a slow building of popular support for rational disarmament positions. More energy should be devoted to internal organization and education than to current appeals to elected representatives. Only a strong organization is capable of altering the political process and precipitating those critical events which could lead to the breakdown of that weak/strong power structure that supports the nuclear arms race.

Another strategy situated outside the political process is the humanization of East-West relations. One of the most fundamental psychological strategies underpinning the nuclear arms race and the Cold War is the psychological manipulation of dehumanization. This phenomenon, studied by members of the International Physicians for the Prevention of Nuclear War, is what I sometimes refer to as the enemy syndrome.

In order to prepare for war against a people, one must dehumanize that people, rendering them into objects. Only then does it become feasible to mobilize vast resources against them and to persuade our population to accept the ultimate sacrifice of nuclear war in order to deter "the enemy". The propaganda war between East and West, and in particular between the United States and the Soviet Union (with Canada as a U.S. appendage), is not ultimately about facts. It is not so much about the weapons themselves (who has the most and of which kind), but concerns the manipulation of psychological images.

Which side is the enemy? Who must be impeded or destroyed? This is the propaganda that stimulates the Cold War. As in any public relations effort, the goal is to create a *general feeling* about the object, as one would about a car or a detergent. This general feeling of hostility toward the enemy as object is then used for practical political and military purposes by the power structure. This psychological manipulation has been extremely successful at every level in Canada, on both masses of population and our elected representatives. Echoes of it are found everywhere.

International Physicians for the Prevention of Nuclear War has suggested that the humanization of East-West relations is perhaps the most important task of the disarmament movement. This can be accomplished only by increasing contacts of a non-governmental nature—scientific, cultural, medical, sporting—between people of Eastern Europe and those of the West. Against the overwhelming propaganda machine of the power structure supporting the nuclear arms race, these contacts must be emphasized and publicized.

The present trend towards annihilation will not be impeded by a rational discourse within the political process. It can be stopped only by an emotional realization that we and our children have no future without disarmament, that the "others" are as human as we are, and that concerted actions—whether acceptable or unacceptable to authority—must be used to precipitate a chain of events which alone can break the political power underlying the arms race.

Directions for the Canadian Peace Movement

Ronald Babin, Eric Shragge, and Jean-Guy Vaillancourt

THE EMERGENCE OF A NEW type of antiwar movement in Canada began in earnest in the early 1980s. Since then this movement has been able to contribute to a rise of consciousness, among a large public, concerning the dangers of the newly accelerated phase of the arms race. It has also helped people understand the urgency of actions to criticize and to counter the militarism that animates our political leaders. Canada has been the theatre of a great number of important activities in favour of disarmament and peace.

As a general rule, however, actions in favour of peace have been characterized by a series of narrow themes that have come and gone. The first target was the signing of the U.S.-Canada umbrella agreements authorizing the United States to test various arms systems on Canadian soil. After that came the struggle against the testing of air-launched Cruise missiles in Alberta. Next was the effort to block Canadian participation in Reagan's Strategic Defense Initiative. And so it goes on. The results of these campaigns did not meet the expectations of the Canadian peace movement. The umbrella agreements were hurriedly signed by Ottawa and Washington and the testing of the Cruise did take place. As for Star Wars, the Progressive Conservative government gave an ambiguous and contradictory answer to the Reagan administration by pronouncing a "no" that is in fact a "yes". Behind a formal refusal to participate officially in a government-to-government accord, the federal government appeared eager to give real support and financial aid to companies and university researchers involved in Star Wars research and development. Furthermore, Canada's military budget has been increasing considerably each year because of the current military modernization policy (new F-18s and frigates, upgrading the DEW line, the creation of firing ranges for airplanes) and because of the increasing integration of Canada into a vast North American military-industrial continentalism.

The peace movement can point proudly to some very important consciousness-raising and mobilization of the Canadian population. But the absence of positive and concrete results demonstrates an urgency to initiate new directions in order to be able to oppose effectively both the new arms race and the militarization of the Canadian economy and society. It is one thing to condemn war or to reject this or that type of armament; it is another to know what to do to stop a dynamic that appears to be leading us, if not automatically towards World War III, at least towards an increase in the number of local wars around the globe.

The opposition to war by the peace movement is a praiseworthy goal in itself, but it does not indicate how and through what means that goal can be achieved. The lack of a concrete program constitutes the key problem of the movement. If these questions remain unanswered, all the good intentions in the world will never bring about disarmament and peace. How can we realistically hope for a reversal of the dynamics of the new Cold War and of the dangers for humanity that accompany it?

There are many issues to face squarely. One is the tendency for our society to make war a sacred act: "If you want peace, prepare for war." We must discover what to counterpose to the logic of militarization. To do this we need to collectively develop a global analysis of contemporary militarism and, within that, of the historic role of Canada.

Developing a collective analysis, long-term alternatives, and successful actions all require a broad alliance of social groups inside and outside the current peace movement. To be credible our alternatives must touch the daily lives of individuals throughout our society and must draw together the diverse social groupings of the peace movement.

This process is difficult and complex. A program or orientation, regardless of how good, that comes from the top will not overcome present weaknesses. For an alternative perspective to be effective, it must take hold within local disarmament committees, in neighbourhoods, in the workplace, in educational institutions, and as part of the activities of numerous popular groups and movements. This is a long process, but backing away from contentious issues can lead nowhere except to discouragement and frustration after each dead-end campaign runs its course.

It is important, then, to consider carefully the movement's approach to both questions of peace and disarmament and issues of action and organization, and to weigh the possibilities of alternative approaches. These alternative approaches, if widely adopted, could move the movement in a radical direction; yet they are based on three basic assumptions that flow out of the demands and goals of those in the peace movement who share a more traditional or moderate viewpoint.

The Push to Unilateral Initiatives

The first assumption is that disarmament will not occur through multi-lateral or bilateral talks of world leaders left to their own devices. The history of these talks has been nothing short of disaster. If anything, they have acted to rationalize and more systematically perpetuate the arms race.[1] In order to break the reciprocal arms game played by both blocs, clear unilateral steps or independent initiatives are required.[2] This position does not imply the simplistic casting off of all weapons. This is perhaps desirable, but it is politically unrealistic without serious defence alternatives.[3] As Dan Smith and Ron Smith argue:

> It would be a contradiction in terms to rely for the first steps, or at any stage in disarmament, on the actions of those who manage and benefit from the international military order. They are part of the problem which the disarmament movement sets out to solve. A political approach to disarmament which relies on their actions in diplomatic negotiations is simply turning aside from the main political impetus towards disarmament in the mass movements. This is perhaps the fundamental rationale for opting for unilateral measures of disarmament. The fabric of the military order will not come apart smoothly and simultaneously across all countries.[4]

Specific actions are required to break the momentum of the arms race. The disarmament movement must demand that unilateral steps be taken without regard for reciprocity. There are enough arms, and the peace movement should not fall into the deadly trap of balance and the numbers game. Each bloc can easily afford to take steps in the direction of disarmament without any real threat to its "security". The concept of overkill, used so often in the movement, is the key in defending unilateral initiatives. The politics of the power blocs is the enemy. To demand bilateral or multilateral talks reinforces the legitimacy of these politics. The disarmament movement must see itself in basic opposition to the system of states and power relations that generates the arms race. Its demands must reflect this opposition and its activists need not worry about how the state system negotiates. The concern of the movement in any country is to push as hard as possible on its own government and to create the international solidarity needed to support independent initiatives.

Demands for unilateral initiatives are not new to the peace movement. Demands for no Cruise or to stop the MX are unilateral. It can be argued, and indeed it is by the right, that this position is pro-Soviet. The rejoinder to this criticism is quite simple: We demand unilateral action on all sides. But since we live under the North American defence umbrella, our main focus must be the problem here at home in North America. Unilateral steps can only promote more effective talks for arms limitation agreements. Waiting for bilateral or multilateral action postpones forever any real possibility of breaking the momentum and irrationality of the arms race.

In order to apply the principle of unilateralism, we also require a definition of Canada's role in the arms race and in bloc politics. Canada, through the Defense Production Sharing Arrangement and other treaties, is virtually integrated into the U.S. military-industrial complex. The ideology that underpins this integration is that we share a common enemy with the United States: the USSR and "world communism". The peace movement must challenge both the role Canada plays and the assumptions of this ideology in order to break the credibility and legitimacy of the superpowers. By providing an example middle powers can weaken the hold of bloc politics and reduce the strength of the two superpowers. Canada can set an important example of the road to peace by removing itself unilaterally from bloc politics and reducing its contribution to the production of weapons and other military waste. If nations move independently, then and only then can the grips of both the United States and the USSR be loosened.

Non-Alignment and Opposition to Bloc Politics

A second assumption is that the disarmament movement should be non-aligned. It must advocate positions and policies that do not serve and are critical of both superpowers and their respective blocs. In each country the movement must push its own government in the direction of non-alignment.

A major conflict exists in the movement between those who support the concept of non-alignment and those who support pro-Soviet politics through the various affiliates of the World Peace Council. Beyond the many political, theoretical, and historical reasons for non-alignment[5] there is a simple, tactical reason to support it. A movement that in the long term is not able to transcend the bloc politics cannot retain public credibility. The fears of the general public about the Soviet threat are very real. In order to counter these perceptions, a critique—and certainly an understanding—of Soviet militarization and its role in the world is required.

Clearly, the Soviets are not going to invade Canada; their tanks in Eastern Europe are designed for local consumption rather than for the invasion of the West. Yet a critique of Soviet society is necessary in order to reveal the reciprocal nature of the bloc system and the specific role played by the USSR. The non-aligned movement, however, should not fall into the trap of playing on media-supported, knee-jerk, cold warriorism, with all the legitimacy this trap gives to the right and red-baiters in the West.[6]

In this way, a credible critique can be made of both superpowers and their historical, reciprocal relationship. Another concrete way to move in this direction is to link support for individual liberties, particularly in the independent peace movements in Eastern bloc countries.[7] This position has been the one feature that has separated the non-aligned from the pro-Soviet peace movements. The link between increased militarism in the West and repression in the East cannot be ignored, and in the long term making this link is the only way to build true international solidarity and achieve the goal of establishing the peace movement as an international people's movement. The European movement has taken some strides in this direction. "Detente from below" is no longer only about the support of independent peace activists in the East by those in the West, but also about the building of a common vision through dialogue about the nature of a united, independent Europe.[8]

The peace movement defines its orientation along the lines of a non-aligned Europe. Although the political forces necessary to bring about this goal at this time are remote, it is clear that non-alignment is on the political agenda. In a sense, the deployment of U.S. missiles in Europe backfired. Instead of consolidating U.S. power in Europe, it undermined its credibility and support. In Canada, given our integration with the United States, the possibility of non-alignment may seem even more distant. However, just as the peace movement should be critical of both the U.S. and the USSR, it needs to advance long-term alternatives for Canadian foreign and military policy. The underpinning of these alternatives is non-alignment.

If the peace movement does not raise these options, they will not be raised. Further, its own credibility depends on putting forward new alternatives. The argument that Canada plays a peaceful role in the world should be used as a means of introducing the policy of non-alignment to public debate and consciousness, by demanding that Canada actually play a constructively peaceful role, particularly through example.

Non-alignment has specific implications in the Canadian context for both foreign policy and economic development. Non-alignment would imply not only a break with U.S.-dominated foreign policy. But because Canada is economically intermeshed with the U.S. a basic redefinition of these relations would be required. Canada has been a supporter of U.S. policies and a loyal NATO member.[9] It has been less shrill as a cold warrior, but very cautious in its criticisms of U.S. foreign policy. Canada, as a junior partner in NATO, has supported NATO policies on nuclear weapons. Although the air-launched Cruise missile is not part of any NATO obligation, the government used its commitment to NATO as justification to test the Cruise in Canada. Trudeau defended his policy by arguing that it gave Canada credibility in the eyes of both superpowers.

Clearly, a central issue for the peace movement is Canada's adherence to the logic of bloc politics. The Canadian peace movement can learn from the European movement where NATO itself has come under increasing attack. This direction is essential to break the momentum of the arms race.

Opposition to Conventional Weapons and Intervention

A third assumption is that the issues of conventional and nuclear weapons are not separable. Much of the support received by the peace movement comes because of the uncontrolled growth of nuclear weapons and the related tensions between the superpowers. These pose an extreme threat to humanity. At the same time, opposition to conventional weapons must be given prominence in the disarmament movement.

One reason is that the defence establishments, particularly NATO and that of the United States, link conventional and nuclear weapons into an integrated military strategy. Several antinuclear arms spokespeople have correctly argued that nuclear weapons are essentially unuseable; yet, in their place they wish to substitute conventional weapons.[10] One reason for the possibility of this shift is a result of changes in these weapons. Michael Klare points out that new conventional weapons are more and more similar to tactical nuclear weapons in their destructive capacity, their interchangeability with nuclear warheads, and their accuracy.[11] These sophisticated weapons have played an increasingly prominent role in local conflicts in the Third World, in Lebanon, for example, or the Falklands or the war between Iraq and Iran. Their destructive capacity, which far exceeds previous generations of weapons, has changed the orientation to battlefield warfare.[12]

In opposing conventional arms the peace movement can speak out against intervention into the Third World nations and against their militarization. Fred Halliday proposes four major reasons to oppose both nuclear and conventional arms:

    i) ...an objection to military spending and the use of force must cover the Third World as much as it covers the developed countries, since the moral and economic costs apply there as much as anywhere;

    ii) ...the very buildup in nuclear weapons...is designed for use in Third World crisis situations;

    iii) ...for all the focus on nuclear weapons, the current arms race and arms buildup primarily involve conventional weapons for use in the Third World;

    iv) ...if there is going to be a Third World War, it is most likely that it will be brought about by a great power confrontation over a Third World crisis spot.[13]

The peace movement in its program of action and analysis must take these questions far more seriously. It needs to move from a single issue antinuclear arms movement to a broader position that includes antimilitarism and Third World solidarity.

Another reason why the issue of conventional weapons is critical for the Canadian peace movement is closer to home. One of Canada's central, and expanding, military roles is its production of conventional weapons, mainly for export. Canadian industry is integrated with the U.S. military-industrial complex through the Defense Production Sharing Arrangement and receives ever larger subsidies from the Canadian Defence Industry Productivity Program.[14] The demands for military production, both as part of Canada's membership in NATO and its "special" relationship to the U.S., increasingly defines other aspects of daily life, such as the structure of the labour market, training and research demands, and the role of high technology. The arms race touches questions of unemployment, education, and in the longer term the demands for increasing secrecy and state security. The negative economic consequences of the arms production include unstable employment and the sacrifice of social programs in order to contribute to military related production.[15]

In order to counter these trends, the peace movement has begun to systematically advance a program of economic conversion.[16] Proposals to convert from military to socially-useful production have been used to counter the argument that military production produces jobs. Peace activists cite evidence that other forms of state or private spending generate more per dollar than the military.[17]

Once these points are made, however, there are other problems. For conversion to take place the specifics of each plant—its machinery, level of technology, labour force—need to be analysed to see if conversion is feasible. In other words, it is not obvious from a technical viewpoint that it is worthwhile to convert all military industry. As well, the military industries are privately owned and operated by large corporations. Thus, even if conversion is both technically feasible and socially desirable for job creation, why would private corporations give up a profit-making enterprise? Capitalists invest in the arms race because they expect to make profit. For them to convert their plants, alternative products must promise at least the same level of profitability. Conversion is a good argument to make, yet it implies a direct attack on the traditional prerogatives of capital, including the right to determine what products are produced.

Campaigns of "Jobs with Peace" are another avenue. Linking demands for socially-useful employment (particularly through state spending) presents wider options and avoids the technical and private sector issues linked to conversion. At another level, and in the longer term, conversion should be seen not only at the level of the factory, but in the context of a more general alternative economic policy designed to provide high levels of employment with socially-useful work, respect for the ecosystem, and links to neighbourhood or community needs under worker management. We need to go beyond the argument that the arms race produces jobs but non-military production produces more. We must link economic development and disarmament with ecology, employment, and Third World relations. If the peace movement takes up these positions, it will clearly enter a broader political and social debate and challenge fundamental social relations in Canadian society.

Alternatives and Counter-Power

Developing such an analysis implies that the peace movement must study the functioning of the economic and political systems in order to understand and challenge the militarization of society. It is important to develop a historical and critical analysis of the numerous changes that are occurring in our advanced industrial societies and in the rest of the world. This analysis would enable us to distinguish what is desirable and what is not, and what is inevitable and what can be changed. This would allow us to formulate realistic alternatives to militarization and to the underlying socio-economic and political crises which are responsible for war.

This type of analysis also helps us avoid images of a peaceful utopia that will fall on us out of the blue. It helps us discover a different road to disarmament and peace. It popularizes the idea that there is not only one particular goal to be reached. Rather there is something much broader at stake concerning a mode of development, the choice of a type of society, and the manner in which both of these could be attained. Such an evaluation reveals the powerful and organized interests that defend the status quo. It will be necessary to challenge these interests along the road to disarmament and peace.

This analytical process will raise the collective knowledge of the peace movement in order to stimulate a better understanding of the conflictual nature of the struggle for peace and to facilitate the identification of the social groups, the methods, and the actions that have the best chance of bringing about the desired transformation.

The peace movement is characterized by its denunciation of the increasing nuclearization and militarization of the world. But if we examine the situation more closely, we discover that what we have is really a mobilization against those in power. This power elite proposes and imposes a mode of development based increasingly on the arms race between the East and West. This type of exercise of power has numerous facets that transcend regions and countries to concern the planet as a whole. This indicates the limits to a policy that looks at one narrow question. We need to focus instead on the kind of counter-power that must be mobilized against the militarization of the international economy and polity. This counter-power must be utilized to resist the capacity of control that this system has on the life of entire populations, a capacity of control that culminates in its ability to exterminate all human life.

The peace movement cannot avoid a profound and sustained reflection on the alternatives that could limit this military-industrial and technocratic power. Technocratic power is based on the capacity to reduce every political and social problem to its technical expression, and to impose on them, through the appeal to "experts", an answer that is purely technological (a technical fix). The case of Reagan's Strategic Defense Initiative illustrates well this increasing dimension of the present-day exercise of power.[18] The boundaries and limits of technocratic power need to be understood. Against notions of technocratic power our counter-power will develop through an exploration of a variety of possibilities, such as detente from below, non-alignment, non-provocative defence, conscientious objection, non-nuclear defence, conflict resolution, non-violent civil defence, transarmament, demilitarized zones, nuclear-free zones, alternative alliances, and alternative dialogues.

Towards an Extra-Parliamentary Opposition

Moderates in the peace movement have put their emphasis on parliamentary lobbying, hoping this will be an adequate mechanism for change. Such a hope indicates a naive and false analysis of the state and the processes of social change. One main goal for the development of a social movement must be to retain its autonomy from the state, which has the proven ability to define, co-opt, and manipulate its opposition. This implies that the peace movement must develop its extra-parliamentary standing, and not be dragged into the limited debates of the political arena as a primary focus.

The question that arises is how will change take place if not through attempts to influence political leaders? Certainly, any social movement wants to influence political leaders, but must also raise the issue of power. The state is essentially about relations of power. What is required is nothing less than a social movement that acts outside of parliament as a serious oppositional force.

Some activists within the traditional socialist or social democratic currents argue that the main way to bring about meaningful change is through the election of a left party. The problem with this is that the only large Canadian party that has what approaches a progressive position on disarmament is the New Democratic Party, a party that will not have sufficient parliamentary weight in the foreseeable future to push for major changes. Even if it had the weight, we would question its political will to make significant changes. The history of social democratic parties in power is filled with examples of backsliding and abandonment of principle, particularly when it comes to confronting fundamental power relations. The track record of these parties in power has been one of support or at best moderately compromised support for nuclear arms. The French Socialist Party supports an independent deterrence, and until recently West Germany's social democrats supported Cruise and Pershing II. There are real possibilities for achieving power in Britain, but given the tendency of the parliamentary Labour Party to compromise either during election campaigns or in office, it is uncertain that a Labour victory by itself would bring the desired results even with its progressive party program on these issues.[19] The crucial ingredient in this scenario is the extra-parliamentary movement, which can push an elected party to carry through its program and support it against right-wing counter-attack.

A movement carries the message for disarmament by changing the overall social and political environment on this issue. It debates and discredits opposing arguments, so that neither the government in power nor traditional supporters such as the press can advocate positions supporting the arms race. This has occurred to an extent on the issue of limited nuclear war, a ridiculous concept, which political leaders have been forced to drop from public discussion—although it is still officially part of NATO and U.S. policy.

One role of a peace movement, then, is educational. It must fully discredit the opposition's arguments on a large scale and in the mainstream of social life. Educational events, pamphlets, public debates should all be part of movement activity.

The movement needs to involve very large numbers in order to be effective. This does not only mean annual demonstrations, but a continual involvement within society's mainstream. The activity includes not only the traditional sources of opposition, such as trade unions and other popular groups, but also the establishment of disarmament groups in neighbourhoods, workplaces, social groups, and religious organizations. The problem of how radical these groups will become is less important initially; what is more important is that the issues get discussed widely, and that action in opposing at least some facets of the arms race begins in a wide variety of settings.

The actions of the movement must also be destabilizing. In practice this implies that state and corporate business cannot be carried out as usual. The movement must introduce an element of non-violent uncertainty into daily life. This not only includes the limited and largely symbolic forms of civil disobedience, such as occurred at Litton Industries, but also extends to wider measures, including boycotts, strikes, and tax resistance, which disrupt the normal functioning of corporations and the state.

These are the types of power-levers that the peace movement has access to due to our numbers, our positions in the division of labour, and our power as consumers. Through public education the movement must ensure that a wide range of people will feel that these kinds of powerful tactics are justified, and that these people will be willing to participate. Ideologically, the movement should work towards discrediting institutions, such as NATO, and Canada's relationship with the United States. To some extent this process has begun with the European movement's challenges to NATO.

If the movement is successful in these tasks, the government will surely respond. It may find it necessary to make concessions in order to maintain public credibility; it can produce limited compromises to try to co-opt and demobilize the more moderate sections of the movement; or it can try to use repression. The task is to create a situation in which the government of the day faces a crisis of confidence and is forced to make concessions. The Canadian movement is a long way from that point. Lobbying the state in the way suggested by moderates will not get us there. Only an extra-parliamentary movement can accomplish the enormous tasks that may result in a more peaceful world.

The specific tactics chosen by groups and organizations are less important in the context of an extra-parliamentary approach. The key question is whether or not any specific action or event can bring in new people, push forward the debate, and educate others. Mass demonstrations provide an opportunity to show the extent of opposition to the arms race, to conduct extensive public education in the process of mobilization, and to generate a sense of participation in an international movement. They give encouragement to those working on smaller, isolated projects. Smaller actions, such as the non-violent actions at Litton Industries, may raise specific questions and sharpen public understanding of Canada's role in the arms race.

The range of possible tactics is enormous, and each has a place as part of a decentralized social movement. The major point is that local activity must be supported and encouraged. There is some danger, for instance, in the formation of a national peace alliance if activities of this alliance overshadow and remove initiatives from the base. The movement will only be strong if there is activity at the base involving and informing people directly and making links with other local movements—feminists or trade unionists, for example.

The question of organizing larger, broader campaigns is an immediate concern to some. The success of the 1985 Shadow Project on Hiroshima Day in cities around the world points to the possibilities of co-ordinating actions from below. Groups organized themselves locally to paint shadows on streets commemorating the victims of the first atomic bomb. The large numbers of participants were co-ordinated through communications between groups on a horizontal basis.

The question of organization is closely related to the idea of locally initiated actions. To be effective the movement has to draw together the diverse local activities, yet in such a way as not to undermine their own programs. Smaller units create an opportunity to develop anti-sexist and anti-hierarchical organizational structures. The best form of organization would appear to be federations, with delegates chosen and decision-making power and accountability resting with smaller units. Obviously there are tensions in this form of organization, but it is the form that can encourage local autonomy, decentralized activity, and in the longer term maintain the extra-parliamentary orientation necessary for the peace movement.

Building the Movement

The Canadian peace movement is a complex movement. It is regionally fragmented and its members represent a huge range of differences of political ideology, class, sex, age, nationality, and vision of social and economic development. Although it is somewhat risky and problematic to categorize peace groups, these differences do seem to represent two major tendencies, related in turn to two different political cultures and kinds of logic. The first tendency favours developing a more strictly political movement and looks to the trade unions and left-wing political parties for support. The second tendency, with a wider conception of the movement, seeks to come together with progressive social forces to put forward a socio-political critique and to work out an alternative to today's militarist, productivist society.

There is some distance between these two points of view, but they are not completely irreconcilable. Each tendency is a significant component of the peace movement; each needs the other's support. Wide grassroots support is needed for a political initiative of any consequence. On the other hand, new life in the political sphere is necessary to spread and concretely develop the desire for an alternative society. For us the key issue is a convergence between the two tendencies.

In Canada as elsewhere, the antiwar movement is a huge laboratory where a variety of personalities, experiences, and ideas are brought together. It brings together various social movements, ecologists, feminists, Christian activists, international solidarity groups, popular groups, and the like. And it provides the context in which trade unions and some left-wing political groups can work to integrate alternative ideas into their political thinking.

At this stage, it is hard to measure the impact of the convergence between the two tendencies. However, this convergence is an indication of what is new in the current movement for disarmament and peace and of how it has broken with the past. The movement represents a genuinely new kind of pacifism that is significantly different from the more strictly political and issue-oriented models represented by the ban-the-bomb movement of the fifties and sixties and the movement against the Vietnam War of the sixties and seventies. It is a synthesis of these earlier movements with the new social movements of the seventies, which were formed to resist the technocratic view of a society and to develop radical alternatives based on self-management. These movements not only challenge militarism and the industrial policies that feed it. But they also hope to achieve something more permanent than previous movements did, to resist new forms of domination, and to build a vast movement for social emancipation.

The new antiwar movement in Canada is thus an expression of the desire of non-aligned progressive forces to join with the most dynamic elements of the trade union movement in building a genuine common front that can resist the strengthening of technocratic and military power and work out viable, attractive alternatives.

The evolution of the two major currents coexisting in the Canadian peace movement will greatly influence the struggle for disarmament and peace in Canada. The key question is how the various regional and social components inside the movement will continue to work together, and how the movement will succeed in becoming a more representative and efficient political voice. The two major tendencies could converge if the movement is willing to take the time and the effort to reflect on the desired meaning of its actions, and to develop a socio-economic and political analysis concerning the questions of defence, of security, of militarization, of disarmament and of peace.

We must seek to understand the roots of war in order to mobilize greater numbers of people and to build their capacity to act effectively over the long run to meet our goals of disarmament and world peace.

Notes

1. See Jane Sharpe, "Is Arms Control Finally Bankrupt?", *END Journal*, Issue 8, February-March 1984. For a more general discussion see Alva Myrdal, *The Game of Disarmament* (New York, 1982).

2. For an in-depth discussion on unilateralism, see Dimitrios Roussopoulos, ed., *Our Generation Against Nuclear War* (Montreal, 1983), section on unilateralism, pp. 199-224.

3. For a discussion of non-violent defence, Roussopoulos, *Our Generation Against Nuclear War*, pp. 261-302; Gene Sharp, *Exploring Non Violent Alternatives* (Boston, 1971); and for more conventional alternatives see Ben Danklarr, "In Defense of the Realm," *END Journal*, Issue 9, April-May 1984, pp. 18-20.

4. Dan Smith and Ron Smith, *The Economics of Militarism* (London, 1983), pp. 117-118.

5. See E.P. Thompson, *Beyond the Cold War* (New York, 1982); and Bryan Palmer's article in this book.

6. See, for example, Barrie Zwicker, "USSR: Media Treatment," in *Briarpatch*, Vol. 13, No. 2, March 1984, pp. 20-21.

7. For an ongoing discussion of the independent peace movements in Warsaw Pact countries, see *END Journal*, and related pamphlets.

8. See George Konrad, *Anti-Politics* (London, 1984), and chapter in this book by Babin, Beaudet, and Shragge.

9. See Palmer's chapter in this book for a discussion of Canada and NATO.

10. See McGeorge Bundy, George F. Kennan, Robert S. MacNamara, Gerard Smith, "Nuclear Weapons and the Atlantic Alliance," *Foreign Affairs*, Summer 1982.

11. Michael T. Klare, "The Inescapable Links: Interventionism and Nuclear War," *Our Generation*, Vol. 15, No. 3, pp. 7-10; and Michael T. Klare, "The Return to Conventional Weapons," in *World View 1984* (New York, 1983), pp. 61-75.

12. See Randall Forsberg et al., *The Deadly Connection: Nuclear War and U.S. Intervention* (American Friends Service Committee, 1983).

13. Fred Halliday, "Exporting the Cold War," *END Journal*, Issue 8, February-March 1984, p. 28.

14. See Ernie Regehr, "Canada as a Nuclear-Weapons-Free-Zone," in Ernie Regehr and Simon Rosenblum, eds., *Canada and the Nuclear Arms Race* (Toronto, 1983); and Ernie Regehr, "The Reagan Boom Years: Military Production in Canada," *Ploughshares Monitor*, Vol. IV, No. 4, Institute of Peace and Conflict Studies, Conrad Grebel College, University of Waterloo.

15. See Smith and Smith, Chapter 4, "The Economic Consequences of Military Spending," in *The Economics of Militarism*.

16. For a discussion of conversion, see Smith and Smith, Chapter 5, "The Economics of Disarmament," in *The Economics of Militarism*; Hilary Wainwright and Dave Elliot, *The Lucas Plan: A New Trade Unionism in the Making?* (London, 1982); and P. Aronoff, P. Bonnet, M. Jacques, Y-Y Rompre, and S. Stillitz, "L'emploi dans le naval au Quebec: A grand la véritable relance?", CSN, Montreal, Quebec.

17. See figures, for example, cited in "Les Usines d'Armement au Quebec" and Smith and Smith, *The Economics of Militarism*.

18. See "The Basic Ideology of the Nuclear Establishment", in R. Babin, *The Nuclear Power Game* (Montreal, 1985), pp. 95-106.

19. For a discussion of that long history see Ralph Miliband, *Parliamentary Socialism* (London, 1972).

Bibliography

1. Books

Babin, Ronald, *The Nuclear Power Game*, Montreal, Black Rose Books, 1985, 236 pp.

Bahrs, R. et al., *The Dynamics of END*, Nottingham, University Paperbacks, 1981.

Bertell, Rosalie, *No Immediate Danger: Prognosis for a Radioactive Earth*, Toronto, Women's Press, 1985, 435 pp.

Canadian Peace Listing (1984 edition), Directory of over 500 Canadian Peace Organizations, 5851 Durocher, Outremont, Quebec, H2V 3Y5.

Capra, Fritjof and Charlene Spretnak, *Green Politics: The Gobal Promise*, New York, E.D. Dutton Inc., 1984, 244 pp.

Cook, Alice and Gwyn, Kirk, *Greenham Women Everywhere: Dreams, Ideas and Actions from the Women's Peace Movement*, London, Pluto Press, 1983, 128 pp.

Die Grünen, *Programme of the German Green Party*, London, Heretic Books, 1983, 54 pp.

Endicott, Stephen, *James G. Endicott: Rebel Out of China*, Toronto, University of Toronto Press, 1980, 421 pp.

Giangrande, Carole, *The Nuclear North: The People, the Regions, and the Arms Race*, Toronto, Anansi, 1983, 231 pp.

Gorz, André, *Ecology as Politics*, Montreal, Black Rose Books, 1982, 215 pp.

Harding, Bill, *Uranium Mining in Northern Saskatchewan*, Regina, Regina Group for a Non-Nuclear Society, 1979, 87 pp.

Hunter, Robert, *Warriors of the Rainbow: A Chronicle of the Greenpeace Movement*, New York, Holt, Rinehart and Winston, 1979, 454 pp. (1st edition).

Johnston, Diana, *The Politics of Euromissiles: Europe's Role in America's World*, London, Verso Books, 1984, 218 pp.

Kaldor, Mary, *The Baroque Arsenal*, New York, Hill and Wang, 1981, 294 pp.

Kelly, Petra, *Fighting for Hope*, Boston, South End Press, 1984, 121 pp.

Knelman, Fred H., *Nuclear Energy: The Unforgiving Technology*, Edmonton, Hurtig Publishers, 1976, 260 pp.

Knewlman, F.H., *Reagan, God and the Bomb*, Toronto, McClelland and Stewart, 1985, 343 pp.

Kovel, Joel, *Against the State of Nuclear Terror*, Montreal, Black Rose Books, 1985, 250 pp.

Leger Sivard, Ruth, *World Military and Social Expenditures 1985*, Washington, World Priorities Publications, 1985, 52 pp.

Levant, Victor, *Quiet Complicity: Canadian Involvement in the Vietnam War*, Toronto, Between The Lines, 1986, 320 pp.

McAllister, Pam (ed.), *Reweaving the Web of Life: Feminism and Non-Violence*, Philadelphia, New Society Publishers, 1982, 440 pp.

Melman, Seymour, *The Politics and Economics of Reversing the Arms Race*, Ottawa, Carleton University Information Services, 1985, 38 pp.

Overy, Bob, *How Effective are Peace Movements?* Montreal, Harvest House, 1982, 78 pp.

Perry, Thomas L. (ed.), *The Prevention of Nuclear War*, Vancouver, Physicians for Nuclear Responsibility (B.C. Chapter), 1984, 335 pp.

Perry, Thomas L. and Dianne De Mille (eds.), *Nuclear War: The Search for Solutions*, Vancouver, Physicians for Social Responsibility, 1985, 324 pp.

Regehr, Ernie, *Making a Killing: Canada's Arms Industry*, Toronto, McClelland and Stewart, 1975, 135 pp.

Regehr, Ernie and Simon Rosenblum (eds.), *Canada and the Nuclear Arms Race*, Toronto, Lorimer, 1983, 268 pp.

Rosenbluth, Gideon, *The Canadian Economy and Disarmament*, Ottawa, Institute of Canadian Studies, Carleton University, 1978, 189 pp.

Roussopoulos, Dimitrios (ed.), *Our Generation Against Nuclear War*, Montreal, Black Rose Books, 1983, 471 pp.

Roussopoulos, Dimitrios (ed.), *The Coming of World War Three*, Vol. 1: *From Protest to Resistance and the International War System*, Montreal, Black Rose Books, 1986, 285 pp.

Sanger, Clyde, *Safe and Sound: Disarmament and Development in the 80's*, Ottawa, Deneau Publishers, 1983, 122 pp.

Thompson, Dorothy (ed.), *Over Our Dead Bodies: Women Against the Bomb*, London, Virago Press, 1983, 253 pp.

Thompson, Edward P. and Dan Smith (eds.), *Protest and Survive*, London, Monthly Review Press, 1981, 216 pp.

Thompson, Edward P., *Beyond the Cold War: A New Approach to the Arms Race and Nuclear Annihilation*, New York, Pantheon Books, 1982, 198 pp.

Thompson, Murray and Ernie Regehr, *A Time to Disarm*, Montreal, Harvest House, 1978, 38 pp.

Wallis, Jim (ed.), *Waging Peace: A Handbook for the Struggle to Abolish Nuclear Weapons*, Toronto, Fitzhenry and Whiteside, 1982, 304 pp.

Ziegler, David W., *War, Peace and International Politics*, Toronto, Little, Brown and Co., 1981, 446 pp. (2nd edition).

2. Articles

Abley, Mark, "Adventures in the Arms Trade: A Canadian Saga", *The Canadian Forum*, Vol. 59, No. 688, April 1979, pp. 6-12.

Abley, Mark, "From Poland to Portugal, the Disarming of Europe", *The Canadian Forum*, Vol. 61, No. 711, August 1981, pp. 7-13.

Abley, Mark, "The Politics of Peace. An Interview with E.P. Thompson", *The Canadian Forum*, Vol. 62, No. 722, October 1982, pp. 6-9, 39-40.

Adams, Ian, "Selling the Bomb: Confessions of a Nuclear Salesman", *This Magazine*, Vol. 16, No. 2, May 1982, pp. 18-19.

Adamson, Edith, "United Nations Special Session: Disarmament! After the Rhetoric What?", *Humanist in Canada*, No. 47 (Vol. 11, No. 4), 1978, pp. 8-9.

Alfsen, E., L. Hogebrink, M. Kaldor and P. Solo, "Freeze and Withdrawal of Nuclear Weapons: A Strategy for Nuclear Disarmament", *Bulletin of Peace Proposals*, Vol. 16, No. 1, 1985, pp. 5-8.

"Assessing the Peace Petition Caravan Campaign", *Canadian Dimension*, Vol. 19, No. 1, March-April 1985, pp. 32-34.

Bacher, John, "The Independent Peace Movements in Eastern Europe", *Peace Magazine*, Vol. 1, No. 9, December 1985, pp. 8-13.

Bates, D.G. et al., "What a Nuclear War Would do to Canada", *The Canadian Forum*, Vol. 63, No. 729, June 1983, pp. 18-21, 25.

Bradbury, Patricia, "Luftwaffe Over Labrador", *This Magazine*, Vol. 19, No. 3, August 1985, pp. 9-11.

Caldicott, Helen, "The Nuclear Danger Diagnosed", *Humanist in Canada*, No. 69 (Vol. 17, No. 2), Summer 1984, pp. 3-6.

Caloren, Fred et al., "Goals and Strategies for the Canadian Peace Movement", *Our Generation*, Vol. 16, No. 1, Summer 1983, pp. 3-9.

"Canadian Churches on Nuclear Weapons", *The Ecumenist*, Vol. 21, No. 6, Sept.-Oct. 1983, pp. 89-94.

Carr, Betsy, "Voice of Women in Brussels", *Status of Women News*, Vol. 8, No. 3, Summer 1983, pp. 18-21.

Chomsky, Noam, "The Drift Towards Global War", *Studies in Political Economy*, No. 17, Summer 1985, pp. 5-31.

Dale, Stephen, "Riding a New Peace Train", *NOW* (Toronto), Vol. 5, No. 5, Nov. 15-20, 1985, pp. 5-6.

Delaunay, David, "The Peace Petition Caravan Campaign: The View From Sudbury", *Canadian Dimension*, Vol. 19, No. 1, March-April 1985, pp. 35-37.

Eckhardt, William, "Attitudes of Canadian Peace Groups", *The Journal of Conflict Resolution*, Vol. 16, No. 3, 1972, pp. 341-352.

Editorial, "Is this the Living END", *Canadian Dimension*, Vol. 15, No. 7, Aug.-Sept. 1981, pp. 2-3.

Editorial, "Open Letter to the Peace Movement", *Canadian Dimension*, Vol. 17, No. 5, November 1983, pp. 2-3.

Editors (A conversation with), "Goals and Strategies for the Canadian Peace Movement", *Our Generation*, Vol. 16, No. 1, Summer 1983, pp. 3-9.

Ellams, Stephen, "Canada and the Arms Race", *Our Generation*, Vol. 15, No. 1, Winter 1982, pp. 26-27.

Epstein, William, "The Trident Nuclear Threat to Canada", *The Canadian Forum*, Vol. 57, No. 678, February 1978, pp. 6-10.

Farlinger, Shirley, "It's Time to Take the Toys from the Boys," *Status of Women News*, Vol. 8, No. 4, Fall 1983, pp. 22-24.

Farlinger, Shirley, "Sister Watch: Halifax 1985", *Peace Magazine*, Vol. 1, No. 4, August 1985, pp. 12-15, 30.

Fink, Bob, "Movement Must Raise Awareness of the 'Shell Game' Arms Negotiations", *Peace Magazine*, Vol. 1, No. 2, April 1985, p. 8.

Fish, Merriel, "Women, Militarism and the Pentagon", *Our Generation*, Vol. 14, No. 4, Summer 1981, pp. 23-27.

Fisher, Sheldon, "On Civil Disobedience", *Humanist in Canada*, No. 73 (Vol. 18, No. 2), Summer 1985, pp. 12-14.

Frank, J.A., M.I. Kelly and T.H. Mitchell, "The Myth of the 'Peaceful Kingdom': Interpretations of Violence in Canadian History", *The Canadian Journal of Peace Studies*, Vol. 15, No. 3, September 1983, pp. 52-60.

Gauthier, Robert, "Hello to Arms!", *The Last Post*, Vol. 6, No. 8, June 1978, pp. 29-33.

Gerard, W., "Nuclear Power: Debate for the '80s", *Maclean's*, Vol. 92, August 20, 1979, pp. 42-47.

Gifford, C.G., "Refuse the Cruise", *Humanist in Canada*, No. 65 (Vol. 16, No. 2), Summer 1983, pp. 10-12.

Glavin, Terry, "Assuring Nuclear War?", *Canadian Dimension*, Vol. 11, No. 5, June 1976, pp. 4-5.

"Goals and Strategies for the Canadian Peace Movement", *Our Generation*, Vol. 16, No. 1, Summer 1983, pp. 3-9.

Gordon, Charles, "Canadian Peace Groups: A Movement and a Force", *Bulletin* (U.N. Association Canada), Vol. 9, December 1983, pp. 12-13.

Grass, Gunter, "The New Barbarism", *Humanist in Canada*, No. 36 (Vol. 9, No. 1), 1976, pp. 16-18.

Gruending, Dennis, "The Saskatchewan Uranium Pool?", *The Canadian Forum*, Vol. 60, No. 703, October 1983, pp. 15-18.

Gudmundson, Fred, "The Saskatchewan Syndrome", *Canadian Dimension*, Vol. 14, July-Aug. 1979, pp. 28-46.

Hackett, R.A., "Massacres and Media: The KAL-007 Story", *Canadian Dimension*, Vol. 17, No. 6, December 1983, pp. 17-19.

Hancock, Ken, "Understanding of History Necessary if Movement is Going to Succeed", *Peace Magazine*, Vol. 1, No. 2, April 1985, pp. 6-7.

Hollands, R. and L. van der Heide, "Protest and Survive: An Interview with E.P. Thompson", *Canadian Dimension*, Vol. 18, No. 6, Dec. 1984-Jan. 1985, pp. 17-22, 32.

Hunter, Bob, "Plutonium in Motion: Uranium and New-World Alchemy", *This Magazine*, Vol. 18, No. 4, November 1984, pp. 29-31.

Jones, Walker, "Ontarians Planning Peace Conference", *Peace Magazine*, Vol. 1, No. 6, September 1985, pp. 29-30.

Joyce, Jim, "Report on the Operation Dismantle Conference—Ottawa, Ontario, Nov. 13-14, 1981", *Our Generation*, Vol. 15, No. 1, Winter 1982, pp. 32-35.

Kilgour, Art, "Uranium Mining: Who Pays, Who Profits?", *Our Generation*, Vol. 14, No. 2, Summer-Fall 1980, pp. 17-21.

Klare, Michael T., "The Inescapable Links: Interventionism and Nuclear War", *Our Generation*, Vol. 15, No. 3, Summer 1983, pp. 7-10.

Kowaluk, Lucia, "Report on June 12", *Our Generation*, Vol. 15, No. 2, Summer 1982, pp. 3-5.

Kowaluk, Lucia, "Peace Action and Central America: What is Being Done?", *Our Generation*, Vol. 16, No. 2, Spring 1984, pp. 15-25.

"Labour and the Peace Movement: All We Are Saying is Give Peace a Chance", *Canadian Labour*, Vol. 28, No. 10, Nov.-Dec. 1983, pp. 16-19.

Laframboise, Donna, "The Politics of the Peace Petition Caravan Campaign", *Canadian Dimension*, Vol. 18, No. 6, Dec. 1984-Jan. 1985, pp. 23-27.

Langille, David, "Strategies for the Canadian Peace Movement", *Canadian Dimension*, Vol. 19, No. 1, March-April 1985, pp. 27-31 (Part 1).

Langille, David, "Strategies for the Canadian Peace Movement", *Canadian Dimension*, Vol. 19, No. 2, May-June 1985, pp. 30-34 (Part 2).

Lee, Don, "No Hot Cargo to Argentina: Disarming the Junta", *This Magazine*, Vol. 14, No. 6, December 1980, p. 17.

Leitner, Gloria, "From the 60's to the 80's: What Has Changed?", *Humanist in Canada*, No. 53 (Vol. 13, No. 2), Summer 1980, pp. 2-7.

Lentner, Howard H., "Foreign Policy Decision Making: The Case of Canada and Nuclear Weapons", *World Politics*, Vol. 29, No. 1, October 1976, pp. 29-66.

MacAdam, Murray, "Canada's Peace Movement Takes Off Like a Rocket", *The Nuclear Free Press*, No. 14, Summer 1982, p. 15.

MacAdam, Murray, "Swords into Plowshares: The Cruise Missile Conversion Project", *The Canadian Forum*, Vol. 62, No. 720, August 1982, pp. 21, 25.

MacAdam, Murray, "Peace Forces Grow Swiftly in Canada", *The Guardian*, Summer 1982, p. 16.

Macpherson, Kay, "The Seeds of the Seventies", *Canadian Dimension*, Vol. 10, No. 8, June 1975, pp. 39-41.

Mahood, E., "Socialists and the Nuclear Power Issue", *Canadian Dimension*, Vol. 13, No. 6, March 1979, pp. 5-7.

Mandel, David and Eric Shragge, "Movement Should Work Towards an End to Canada's Role in NATO", *Peace Magazine*, Vol. 1, No. 3, May 1985, pp. 28-29.

Mansour, Valerie, "Submarines at Shearwater", *This Magazine*, Vol. 19, No. 3, August 1985, pp. 12-14.

Marchand, Gary, "B.C. Provincial Conference a Success", *Peace Magazine*, Vol. 1, No. 8, November 1985, p. 22.

Mohr, Doug, "Peace Movement Needs to Empower People Not Just Educate Them", *Peace Magazine*, Vol. 1, No. 3, May 1985, pp. 27-28.

Morrison, R.W., "Is Canada Peddling Nuclear Bombs Worldwide in the Cruise of Nuclear Reactors (CANDU)?", *Science Forum*, Vol. 10, December 1977, pp. 3-7.

Muntor, Don and Michael Slack, "Canadian Attitudes on Disarmament", *International Perspectives*, July-August 1982, p. 9.

Murtagh, Pat, "Canada Reaches for W. W. III: Canadarm and the 'Winnable War' ", *This Magazine*, Vol. 17, No. 2, June 1983, pp. 34-36.

Naidu, M.V., "Cruise Missiles in Canada", *The Canadian Journal of Peace Studies (CJPS)*, Vol. 15, No. 1, January 1983, pp. i-iv; "Canada, NATO and the Cruise Missile", *CJPS*, Vol. 15, No. 2, May 1983, pp. 1-12; "Economics Behind the Cruise Missile Testing in Canada", *CJPS*, Vol. 15, No. 3, September 1983, pp. 2-20.

"Non Provocative Defense"—An interview, *Peace Calendar*, Vol. 1, No. 4, August 1985, pp. 16-22.

Palmer, Bryan, "Rearming the Peace Movement", *Canadian Dimension*, Vol. 16, No. 5, July-Aug. 1982, pp. 3-6.

Palmer, Bryan, "Marching Once a Year is not Enough", *Canadian Dimension*, Vol. 17, No. 4, September 1983, pp. 30-32.

Pendercrast, Eudora, "Disarm Ontario", *The Peace Calendar*, Vol. 1, No. 5, June 1983, p. 1.

Pendercrast, John, "School Peacegroups", *The Peace Calendar*, Vol. 1, No. 4, May 1983, p. 1.

Penner, Robert, "NATO's Fear: The Dutch Peace Movement", *The Canadian Forum*, Vol. 64, No. 743, November 1984, pp. 14-16.

"Perspectives on the Anti-Nuclear Movement", *The Nuclear Free Press*, Issue 15, Fall 1982, 19 pp., published by Ontario Public Interest Research Group, Trent University, Peterborough, Ont.

Peters, Paul, "The Triumph of Angst: The Green and the Black in Germany", *The Canadian Forum*, Vol. 63, No. 729, June 1983, pp. 14-17.

Petras, James F. and Morris H. Morley, "The New Cold War: Reagan's Policy Towards Europe and the Third World", *Studies in Political Economy*, No. 9, Fall 1982, pp. 5-44.

Regehr, Ernie, "For Canada's Generals, now There's...Dinner with Wine", *The Last Post*, Vol. 6, No. 2, April 1977, pp. 21-25.

Regehr, Ernie, "Disarmament and Hypocrisy", *The Last Post*, Vol. 6, No. 5, November 1977, pp. 11-13.

Regehr, Ernie, "Now It's 'Civilian' Arms Sales", *The Last Post*, Vol. 6, No. 7, April 1978, pp. 10-12.

Regehr, Ernie, "U.N. Tries Again, But the Arms Build Up Continues", *The Last Post*, Vol. 7, November 1978, pp. 20-21.

Regehr, Ernie, "Cashing in on the Arms Boom", *The Canadian Forum*, Vol. 61, No. 711, August 1981, pp. 14-16, 42.

Regehr, Ernie, "From Deterrence to Intimidation: The Changing Role of Nuclear Weapons", *Our Generation*, Vol. 15, No. 3, Fall 1983, pp. 50-55.

Regehr, Ernie, "The Military Industry in Canada: Street Vendor to the Global Arms Marathon", *Canadian Dimension*, Vol. 19, No. 4, Sept.-Oct. 1985, pp. 16-18, 33.

Robbins, Walter, "Playing Possum with Radioactive Waste", *Canadian Dimension*, Vol. 19, No. 6, Jan.-Feb. 1986, pp. 10, 47.

Robinson, Lukin, "The Arms Race, Inflation and Recession", *The Canadian Forum*, Vol. 62, No. 718, June-July 1982, pp. 12-13.

Rosenblum, Simon, "Canada in the Shadow of the Superpowers", *The Canadian Forum*, Vol. 61, No. 711, August 1981, pp. 17-19.

Rosenblum, Simon, "An Agenda for the Peace Movement", *The Canadian Forum*, Vol. 64, No. 738, April 1984, pp. 18-19.

Roussopoulos, Dimitrios, "On the Nuclear State", *Our Generation*, Vol. 13, No. 4, Fall 1979, pp. 17-20.

Roussopoulos, Dimitrios, "The Politics of the Peace Movement", *Our Generation*, Vol. 15, No. 3, Fall 1982, pp. 3-6.

Seppo, David and Eric Shragge, "The Soviet Union and the Peace Movement: A Response from Montreal to the November 'Open Letter' ", *Canadian Dimension*, Vol. 18, No. 1, March 1984, pp. 17-18.

Sheppard, Michel-Adrien, "Independent Peace Groups in East Germany", *Our Generation*, Vol. 16, No. 1, Summer 1983, pp. 11-19.

Shragge, Eric, "Canada and the Nuclear Arms Race (A Review Essay)", *Our Generation*, Vol. 16, No. 1, Summer 1983, pp. 52-59.

Shragge, Eric, "Cruise: The Test of Canada", *END Journal of European Nuclear Disarmament*, Issue 7, Dec. 1983-Jan. 1984, pp. 23-25.

Shragge, Eric, "Opposing the Canadian War Machine", *Our Generation*, Vol. 16, No. 2, Spring 1984, pp. 2-5.

Shragge, Eric, "Goals Beyond Star Wars", *Peace Magazine*, Vol. 1, No. 11, December 1985, pp. 27-28.

Silva, Edward, "Court Test: The Legality of Nuclear War", *Peace Magazine*, Vol. 1, No. 6, September 1985, p. 29.

Sinn, Hans, "Defense and the Future of Canada", *Humanist in Canada*, No. 66 (Vol. 16, No. 3), Autumn 1983, pp. 15-18.

Sinn, Hans, "Defense Policy Alternatives for Canada", *Humanist in Canada*, No. 67 (Vol. 16, No. 4), Winter 1983/84, pp. 14-16.

Sinn, Hans, "A German Peace Treaty: Demilitarizing Central Europe", *Humanist in Canada*, No. 71 (Vol. 17, No. 4) Winter 1984/85, pp. 5-7.

Sinn, Hans, "The Transformation of War", *Humanist in Canada*, No. 74 (Vol. 18, No. 3), Autumn 1985, pp. 15-17.

Slaughter, Sheila and Metta Spencer, "Interview with Canadian Peace General", *Peace Magazine*, Vol. 1, No. 6, September 1985, pp. 17-22.

Spencer, Metta, "Joanne Young: A Civilly Disobedient Peace Activist", *Peace Magazine*, Vol. 1, No. 1, March 1985, pp. 24-25.

Spencer, Metta, "The Soul of Nonviolence—Interview with Randel Osburn", *Peace Magazine*, Vol. 1, No. 2, April 1985, pp. 11-15.

Spencer, Metta, "Low Level Radiation and Species Death Syndrome—Interview with Rosalie Bertell", *Peace Magazine*, Vol. 1, No. 3, May 1985, pp. 16-23.

Spencer, Metta, "Greenpeace: The Protest in Paradise", *Peace Magazine*, Vol. 1, No. 8, November 1985, pp. 16-18.

Sterling, T.D., "Cover-up at Hanford: The Effects of Low-Dose Radiation", *Humanist in Canada*, No. 52 (Vol. 13, No. 1), Spring 1980, pp. 5-8.

Stewart, Walter, "How Canada Learned to Stop Worrying and Sell the Bomb", *Humanist in Canada*, No. 32 (Vol. 8, No. 1), 1975, pp. 12-16.

Suss, Walter, "Nato and the Warsaw Pact: Armament Insanity vs. Calculated Power", *Telos*, No. 51, Spring 1982, pp. 52-80.

Thompson, Edward, "Notes on Exterminism, the Last Stage of Civilization", *Our Generation*, Vol. 15, No. 1, Winter 1982, pp. 5-25.

Tully, James, "Complex Issues (A Review Essay)", *Our Generation*, Vol. 16, No. 1, Summer 1983, pp. 60-67.

"Two Views on the Canadian Peace Alliance", *Peace Magazine*, Vol. 1, No. 8, November 1985, pp. 26-28.

Wallace-Deering, Kathleen, "Learning to Live with the Russians", *Humanist in Canada*, No. 71 (Vol. 17, No. 4), Winter 1984/85, pp. 8-11.

Waltnertoews, D., "Nuclear Arms Race and the Peace Movement", *Canadian Veterinary Journal*, Vol. 25, No. 5, 1984, pp. 223-225.

Watkins, Mel, "An Economist Looks at the Arms Race", *This Magazine*, Vol. 16, No. 3, July 1982, pp. 15-19.

Wells, MacLean, "Group Politics, Class Politics and the Peace Movement", *Our Generation*, Vol. 15, No. 1, Winter 1982, pp. 29-32.

Westaway, Nina, "Nanoose Campers Petition for Enquiry", *Peace Magazine*, Vol. 1, No. 6, September 1985, p. 30.

Whitaker, Reg, "An Open Letter to Prime Minister Trudeau on the Cruise Missile", *Canadian Dimension*, Vol. 17, No. 5, November 1983, pp. 20-22.

Whitaker, Reg, "What is the Cold War About and Why is it Still with Us?", *Studies in Political Economy*, No. 19, Spring 1986, pp. 7-29.

Williamson, Janice, "Feminism and Civil Disobedience", *The Canadian Forum*, 13, Aug.-Sept. 1984, pp. 13-17.

Wood, Bernard, "Disarmament and Development, Converging Priorities", *Humanist in Canada*, No. 64 (Vol. 16, No. 1), Spring 1983, pp. 30-32.

3. Disarmament and Peace Magazines and Journals

The Activist
c/o Act for Disarmament Coalition
112A Harbord Street
Toronto, Ont.
M5S 1G6

Canadian Peace Alliance News
555 Bloor Street West, Suite 5
Toronto, Ont.
M5S 1Y6

Canadian World Federalist
46 Elgin Street, Suite 32
Ottawa, Ont.
K1P 5K6

The Dismantler
c/o Operation Dismantle
Box 3887, Station "C"
Ottawa, Ont.
K1Y 4M5

EAR News
c/o End the Arms Race
1708 W. 16th Avenue
Vancouver, B.C.
V6J 2M1

Fraser Valley Peace News
16153 - 10th Avenue
Surrey, B.C.
V4A 1A7

Greenpeace Examiner
2623 W. 4th Avenue
Vancouver, B.C.
V6K 1P8

Input/Output
c/o INPUT (Initiative for the Peaceful Use of Technology)
Box 248, Station "B"
Ottawa, Ont.
K1P 6C4

Nanoose Update
#225 - 285 Prideaux Street
Nanaimo, B.C.
V9R 2N2

The Networker
555 Bloor Street West, 2nd Floor
Toronto, Ont.
M5S 1Y6

Newfoundland & Labrador Peace Network News
Box 13392, Station "A"
St. Johns, Nfld.
A1B 4B7

The Nuclear Free Press
Trent University
Peterborough, Ont.
K9J 7B8

Option-Paix
88 Lionel Emond, appt. 3
Hull, P.Q.
J8Y 5S3

Ottawa Peace Calendar
c/o Peace Resource Centre
142 Lewis Street
Ottawa, Ont.
K2P 0S7

Peace Magazine
Box 490, Adelaide Street Station
Toronto, Ont.
M5C 2J6

Peace Meal
c/o Wolfe
Jemseg, N.B.
E9E 1S0

Peace Networker
Box 1527
Lunenburg, N.S.
B0J 2C0

Peace Research. The Canadian Journal of Peace Studies
c/o Brandon University
Brandon, Man.
R7A 6A9

Peace Research Reviews
25 Dundana Avenue
Dundas, Ont.
L9H 4E5

Pigeon Hill Peacemaking
1965 Chemin St-Arnaud
Pigeon Hill, P.Q.
J0J 1T0

Ploughshares Monitor
Institute of Peace and Conflict Studies
Conrad Grebel College
Waterloo, Ont.
N2L 3G6

Quest for Peace. WAND Canada's Quarterly Newsletter
Women's Action for Nuclear Disarmament
233 - 10th Street N.W.
Calgary, Alta.
T2N 1V5

Saskatchewan Peace News
1151 Athol Street
Regina, Sask.
S4T 3C3

Science for Peace Bulletin
University College
University of Toronto
Toronto, Ont.
M5S 1A1

Social Workers for Peace and Disarmament Newsletter
Box 303, Station "T"
Toronto, Ont.
M6B 4A3

Toronto Nuclear Awareness
730 Bathurst Street
Toronto, Ont.
M5S 2R4

Contributors

Phyllis Aronoff is a Montreal activist who has worked in social services, community groups, and the union movement. Her current (and eternal) involvements are feminism and the peace movement.

Ronald Babin is a sociologist who does research at Université de Montréal on social movements. He has written *The Nuclear Power Game* and is active in La Coalition Québecoise Pour le Désarmement et La Paix (CQDP).

Jean-François Beaudet is a graduate student in theology at McGill University interested in the relationship between theological reformulation and non-violence. He is active in Union des Pacifistes du Québec and CQDP.

Pierre Beaudet is a sociologist, and a researcher at Centre d'information et de documentation sur le Mozambique et l'Afrique Australe (CIDMAA), and Centre d'Etudes Arabes pour le Développement (CEAD). He is active in solidarity movements with liberation struggles in the Third World.

Paul Cappon is a physician and sociologist. As a sociologist he has taught at the University of British Columbia and St. Mary's University, Halifax, and authored two books. As a specialist in community medicine, he is now at the Montreal General Hospital and McGill University. He has been active in Canadian and International Physicians for the Prevention of Nuclear War since 1981. He is also the founding president of the Quebec Centre for Nuclear Disarmament and Community Health, a research and educational institute in the public health system of Quebec.

Gordon Edwards is an applied mathematician who teaches at Vanier College in Montreal. He is a co-founder of the Canadian Coalition for Nuclear Responsibility and has consulted on nuclear matters for many government and non-government agencies across Canada.

Leonard Johnson is a retired Major-General in the Canadian forces. He was commandant of the National Defence College 1980-84 and is a member of Generals for Peace and Disarmament, Veterans against Nuclear Arms, the Group of 78, and the Canadian Pugwash Movement.

Marion Kearns is an activist in the peace movement, a long-term member of Voice of Women, Halifax, and a social worker. She was co-ordinator of the International Peace Conference, Halifax, June 1985.

Andrea Levy has an M.A. in history from Concordia University, Montreal. She is a peace activist who co-ordinated a popular peace education project which culminated in a Nuclear Weapons Free Zone referendum in two Montreal communities. She is a member of the executive committee of the Montreal Citizens' Movement.

David Mandel teaches political science at Université de Québec à Montréal, and does research on the role of workers in the 1917 Soviet revolution. He is author of *The Petrograd Workers and the Fall of the Old Regime*, and *The Petrograd Workers and the Soviet Seizure of Power*. He is active in several political and peace organizations.

Bryan Palmer was active in the peace movement in Vancouver at the time of writing the article in this book. He teaches labour history at Queen's University and is the author of a history of the Solidarity movement in British Columbia.

Eric Shragge teaches social policy and community organization at McGill University, School of Social Work. He has written articles and a book on social policy and articles on disarmament. He is active in several disarmament and community organizations.

Dan Smith is Vice-Chairperson, Campaign for Nuclear Disarmament (CND), one of the founders of European Nuclear Disarmament (END), and co-editor with E.P. Thompson of *Protest and Survive.* He is also the author of *Economics of Militarism* (with Ron Smith), *The War Atlas* (with Michael Kidron), and *Fathers' Law.*

Jean-Guy Vaillancourt is Director of the Department of Sociology of Université de Montréal. He is author of *Mouvement Ecologist: Energie et Environnement: Essais d'écosociologie* and *Papal Power.* He edited *Ecologie Sociale et Mouvements Ecologiques* and co-edited "L'Etat et la Société" —two special numbers of *Sociologie et Sociétés,* which he edits. He is active in the CCQDP.

Index

Also available from
Between The Lines

OLD PASSIONS NEW VISIONS
Social Movements and Political Activism in Quebec
Edited by Marc Raboy
Translated by Robert Chodos

The articles in Old Passions New Visions portray a Quebec
that is home to resilient and active social, political, and
cultural movements. Within these movements the questions
of nationalism, feminism, pacifism, labour, and socio-
economic emancipation are being debated and reframed to
meet the new context of the times.

*"This is a worthwhile book. It reminds us just how different the
political landscape of the Quebec nation is from English
Canada's."*
                                                    NOW Magazine

*"The real usefulness of Raboy's book is its role as a forum for
different movements that share a similar political outlook but
remain otherwise separated by language, class, and culture."*
                                                    Montreal Mirror

Please write for a complete list of titles.

Books on the Third World from Between The Lines

Frontyard/Backyard
The Americas in the Global Crisis
Edited by John Holmes and Colin Leys

Quiet Complicity
Canada's Involvement in the Vietnam War
Victor Levant

Children of the Volcano
Alison Acker

South African Women on the Move
The Vukani Makhosikazi Collective

Mirrors of War
Literature and Revolution in El Salvador
Translated with an introduction by Keith Ellis

Jamaica Under Manley
Dilemmas of Socialism and Democracy
Michael Kaufman

Bitter Grounds
Roots of Revolt in El Salvador — 2nd Edition
Liisa North

Gift of the Devil
A History of Guatemala
Jim Handy

Banking on Poverty
The Global Impact of the IMF and the World Bank
Edited by Jill Torrie

Ties That Bind
Canada and the Third World
Edited by Robert Clarke and Richard Swift

Perpetuating Poverty
The Political Economy of Canadian Foreign Aid
Robert Carty and Virginia Smith

Perceptions of Apartheid
The Churches and Political Change in South Africa
Ernie Regehr